THE FIRST DAY OF THE BLITZ

The First Day of the Blitz

September 7, 1940

PETER STANSKY

YALE UNIVERSITY PRESS
NEW HAVEN AND LONDON

For information about this and other Yale University Press publications please contact:

U.S. Office:	sales.press@yale.edu	yalebooks.com
Europe Office:	sales@yaleup.co.uk	www.yalebooks.co.uk

Set in Fournier and Gill Sans by Carnegie Book Production, Lancaster
Printed in Great Britain by St Edmundsbury Press, Bury St Edmunds

Library of Congress Cataloging-in-Publication Data
Stansky, Peter, 1932.
The first day of the blitz: September 7, 1940 / Peter Stansky.
p. cm.
Includes bibliographical references and index.
ISBN 978–0–300–12556–6 (alk. paper) 7944557
1. World War, 1939–1945—England—London. 2. London (England)—History—Bombardment, 1940–1941 I. Title.
D760.8.L7S72 2007
940.54'211—dc22

2007011139

A catalogue record for this book is available from the British Library

10 9 8 7 6 5 4 3 2 1

To my colleagues

Contents

List of Illustrations

Acknowledgments

I AM DEEPLY GRATEFUL to the many who have helped me with this book. I began it at the Stanford Humanities Center, where I held the Violet Andrews Whittier Fellowship. It was a perfect place to work and my fellow Fellows were a very enjoyable and supportive group with whom to spend the year. I was also very grateful for the aid of Dinyar Patel during that time. Since then I have benefited immensely by readings of the manuscript by Susan Groag Bell, Sir Michael Howard, Fred Leventhal, Peter Mandler, and Philippe Tapon. Futhermore, I owe a considerable editorial debt to Sayre Van Young, Trent Duffy and Sally Arteseros. At Yale University Press I am deeply grateful for the enthusiasm of Heather McCallum and, ultimately, for the hard work required by the suggestions she made for revisions. I am also thankful to Rachael Lonsdale, Candida Brazil and Hannah Godfrey in the Press's London office, and the copy-editor Ann Bone. Vivian Wang also helped me immensely. I am very grateful to the staff of the History Department at Stanford University, particularly Paul Navarro; those in Stanford's Library, especially Benjamin Stone; and those who assisted me at the Imperial War Museum and other collections.

I am obliged to the Trustees of the Imperial War Museum for allowing access to the collections, and to each of the copyright holders of unpublished manuscript material. I wish to thank Mr David Allan for the Papers of M. E. Allan, Mr Bruce Gordon-Smith for the Diary of Viola Bawtree, Mrs K.E. Fenlon for the papers of Molly Fenlon, Mr Leslie Jerman for his own material, Mrs A. Regan-Atherton for the Papers of her parents, and Mrs Jean M. Hale for the Papers of her grandmother, Anne J. Shepperd. Every effort was made to trace the copyright owners of other manuscript material, but without success. The author and the Imperial War Museum would be grateful for any information which helps to trace those whose identities or addresses are not currently known.

I am happy to thank the following for kind permission to quote from published copyright material: David Higham Associates on behalf of the Estate of Constantine FitzGibbon for quotations taken from FitzGibbon's *The Blitz* (1957); Curtis, Brown Ltd, London on behalf of the Estate of Sir Winston Churchill, copyright © Winston S. Churchill for excerpts from Churchill's speeches; the Estate of Dorothy L. Sayers and the Watkins/Loomis Agency for Dorothy Sayer's poem 'The English War' (1940); Brian Pollitt, trustee of the Dobb Estate for the words of Barbara Nixon Dobb; and Houghton Mifflin Company and Pan Macmillan for lines from Glyn Maxwell's 'Man Out of the Blue' from Maxwell's *The Sugar Mile: Poems* (2005).

1

The Beginning

"In the perspective of history, the Lesson of London may be that 'Black Saturday', September 7th, 1940 was as significant in its own way – as Bastille Day, July 14th, 1789"

AT TEATIME, or to be precise at 4:14 p.m. on Saturday, September 7, 1940, 348 German bombers – Heinkels, Dorniers and Junkers – and 617 Messerschmitt German fighters crossed the English Channel into British airspace, forming a block 20 miles wide, filling 800 square miles of sky. It was the most concentrated assault against Britain since the Spanish Armada. This was the first day of the London Blitz, which would continue, although with somewhat decreasing numbers of raids after the first two months, until May 10, 1941.

September 7, 1940 marked a transition to a war at a more intense level, and one that would be deeply experienced by the home front. The day was beautiful and unseasonably warm. Then in the late afternoon began 12 hours of horror, punctuated by a brief intermission, first seen as the ending of the raid. The double raid stopped the next day, Sunday, at dawn leaving a severely shaken population. Yet after that first day of heavy bombing there was an acceptance of the situation as well as a determined mobilization in response.

Many recorded their on-the-spot impressions of the beginning of the Blitz. I have drawn on their accounts to convey the feeling of the day, its mixture of ordinariness and terror. Most of these records are in the rich archives of London's Imperial War Museum. These unpublished eyewitness reports are supplemented here by excerpts from published accounts, and they show how "ordinary" people – including London's air raid wardens and firemen – acted and reacted to that day, and set the pattern for the arduous months of bombing that followed. Where appropriate, I have also drawn upon the experiences of writers, artists and other observers.

The Blitz has often been cited as an example of how citizens can withstand attack, draw together and perform heroic actions; certainly this was the case in New York City on September 11, 2001, when the destruction of the World Trade Center's Twin Towers in Manhattan occurred. One of the most frequent comparisons for that day was the London Blitz. The *New York Times* ran quotations from various accounts, particularly from Constantine FitzGibbon's *The Blitz*. The newspaper also published the famous photograph of St Paul's surviving amidst flames, taken on one of the worst days, December 29, 1940, and another of St Paul's captioned "Ground Zero, 1941." Mayor Rudolph Giuliani frequently made comparisons between the events of 9/11 and the Blitz; some even compared his role to that of Churchill. Roy Jenkins, the prominent British politician and a biographer of Churchill, remarked: "What Giuliani succeeded in doing is what Churchill succeeded in doing in the dreadful summer of 1940: he managed to create an illusion that we were bound to win."[1]

In part impelled by 9/11, I wanted to study the Blitz, including "the myth of the Blitz," which most assume emphasizes how well everyone acted under immense strain. Or to put it another way, whether the myth was necessarily totally heroic. I also wanted to examine to what extent the observation by Ritchie Calder was fitting, that September 7 could be compared to Bastille Day as an impetus for changing society. And I wished to investigate whether the assertion by Hugh Dowding, the Air Chief Marshal in charge of Fighter Command during the Battle of Britain, was correct in his assertion that September 7 was "the crucial day" in turning the advantage in the war away from the Nazis. I decided to concentrate on this one day, September 7, 1940.

Though generally associated with London, the Blitz was intensely and tragically experienced elsewhere in Britain as well, including Birmingham, Coventry, Southampton, Manchester, Liverpool, Exeter, Plymouth, and Belfast. Bombs could be dropped almost anywhere, whether deliberately or by chance as the bombers were returning to Germany. The Germans had used aerial bombing before, including, of course, some bombing of London and elsewhere during the First World War. More recently, in 1937, the Germans had carried out a devastating bombing raid in the destruction of the town of Guernica in the Spanish Civil War; the Japanese had bombed China, the Italians Abyssinia. There were bombings and strafing before the Blitz. There had been devastating German raids in September 1939 on Warsaw, and a single highly destructive attack in May 1940 on Rotterdam. But the London experience was much more extensive, days and days of terror from the air from September 1940 until May 1941.

One major purpose of all such bombing for the Germans was to undermine, through the loss of life and property, the morale of the enemy. Bombs would kill approximately 60,000 British civilians by the war's end. (On the worst night of the Blitz – its last, May 10, 1941 – almost 1,500 Londoners died.) The total dead in London by

1. A Heinkel III bomber flying over Wapping and the Isle of Dogs, East London.

war's end was approximately 28,000. The month after the German attacks on Britain ended, the Nazi war machine turned its attention to the invasion of Russia. Later there was the Little Blitz of early 1944 and then the rocket attacks, the V-1s and then V-2s, from June 1944 to March 1945. Until the middle of 1944 there were more British civilian deaths than military.[2] It was unlikely that there was anyone in Britain who did not know of someone who was killed or badly wounded by bombs, or who did not know of places where bombs had fallen. One characteristic the Blitz shares with modern terror is its combination of "ordinariness" with catastrophic events.

The person next door, or oneself, might be at the wrong place at the wrong time, the only requirement being that the area be construed by someone as belonging to an "enemy." During the Second World War, practically anywhere you might be in Britain, and certainly anywhere you might travel, it was possible, with varying degrees of likelihood, that a bomb might fall on you or fall nearby.

It seems to me that this arbitrariness is one central essence of terror, shared by the Blitz and its contemporary form. New York's Twin Towers had been attacked before, yet there was presumably little assumption that they would be targeted again. The Spanish commuters in Madrid in March 2004 had little reason to think that they would be attacked, despite Spanish support of the United States in Iraq. (Of course recent tsunamis, hurricanes and earthquakes have reminded us that nature is a terrorist, claiming far more innocent victims than the 9/11 attacks. But lacking human agency, except in the sense of failures to prepare, there is no human to blame.) It is extremely unlikely that a terrorist act will take place where one just happens to be at a particular time. But the vital point about terror is that it is not beyond the bounds of possibility. In Britain, the Blitz was an example, I believe, of terror on a major scale in a modern way as a work by human beings. Anyone who was in London at the time was potentially vulnerable.

Terror bombing was not, however, a new idea. The Bulgarians may have launched the first such air raids, not very effective, against civilians in the siege against the Turks at Adrianople in 1912.[3] Or one year earlier the Italians had bombed an oasis in Tripoli. Civilians had been bombed in the First World War. The first German bomb dropped on England had been on Christmas Eve 1914, when a single German aeroplane did so on the town of Dover and broke some glass. That year too Germany bombarded Britain by sea. On September 2, 1916 there was the worst Zeppelin raid on

London and there were quite a few other small raids, killing in total 1,239 British during the First World War.[4] The British themselves had bombed Jalalabad and Kabul in Afghanistan in 1919. They pioneered using air power to control insurgent tribes in Iraq in the 1920s. In the same period the French bombed Tetouan in Morocco and also Damascus and areas in Libya.

Cumulatively, such episodes led civilians in the 1930s and early 1940s to the realization that they were vulnerable, that they were potential victims. A city being bombed meant that anyone in it might be killed or wounded by chance. At the same time, since such a fate had a degree of arbitrariness, on the whole one had no choice but to conduct one's life as if it couldn't really happen. One could only take reasonable precautions. In the British case, quite a few left London for the safer countryside. With the outbreak of the war in September 1939, many children were evacuated from the metropolis. However, by the time of the Blitz a year later, there had been so few raids that quite a few of the young evacuees had returned to the city.

The clichés of British character were well suited, on the whole, to deal with this situation: cheerful or rather perhaps ironic, with indeed a possibly cranky stoicism or fatalism. It is striking that the words the British Prime Minister, Tony Blair, used on July 7, 2005, the day of the terror bombing in London, were similar to those used during the Blitz. He talked about the "stoicism and resilience" of the British, saying that they would not be cowed or frightened, that their resolve would not be weakened, that he relied on their "spirit and dignity," their "quiet and true strength." And he vowed that "we will not be terrorized."[5] A few days later he asserted, "If London could survive the Blitz, it can survive four [the number of bombs] miserable events like this."[6]

II

Preparing for War

"Men tend their gardens undisturbed"

THE STORY of September 7, 1940, the first day of the Blitz, begins more than a decade earlier, with the formation of the Air Raid Precaution (ARP) Committee in 1924. British officials, having seen air power begin to come into its own in the First World War, now subscribed to the doctrines of the Italian military theorist Giulio Douhet, who believed that air forces, and air attacks, would win wars in the future. Among the committee's first duties was preparing a report on how to alert the population to raids, and the necessity to have squadrons of bombers and fighting planes. There would need to be a structure of command to prepare for the civil defences against air raids.

In 1927 Lord Thomson, who had been Secretary of State for Air in the Labour government of 1924, remarked that as a result of air raids "both victors and vanquished would be left with ruined cities, widespread distress among the masses of the people, hospitals filled with the maimed and the mutilated of all ages and both sexes, asylums crowded with unfortunate human beings whom terror had made insane."[1] On November 10, 1932 the Prime Minister, Stanley Baldwin, famously said in the House of Commons that "the bomber will always get through. The only defence is offence, which means that you will have to kill more women and children more quickly than the enemy if you want to save yourselves." This was not a plea for more bombers but rather pointing out what would be the horrors of war. Ironically his dramatic statement was taken, depending on the proclivities of the listener, as a plea for either rearmament or disarmament.

The bitter experiences of the First World War had inclined many to pacifism, as one way of avoiding war at almost any cost. And while the government's ARP committee continued to take seriously the high danger of air raid attack, especially on London, its activities were severely restrained by the pressure to spend as little money as possible in the wake of the Depression, particularly on rearmament. Furthermore, the victory of a Labour Party pacifist in the famous East Fulham by-election in October 1933 was widely taken to indicate, despite Hitler's coming to power in Germany in January of that year and Germany's subsequent withdrawal from the Disarmament Conference, that preparations for war were very much out of favour with the electorate.[2]

Given the government's need to economize wherever possible, one reason air power was relatively attractive was its cheapness compared to the army and the navy. Before rearming, the Royal Air Force had to make a series of tough, strategic decisions. How much to spend on new planes? Should the emphasis be on building bombers, which could attack the enemy, or fighters, which could defend the air space over Britain?

By the mid-1930s, there was a considerable body of opinion that the bombing of London and elsewhere would be devastating. To the degree that it did rearm in the first half of the decade, the Royal Air Force emphasized bombers, which the air staff favoured. Focusing on the need to protect the homeland, most politicians pushed for more fighters. In the long run, the politicians would turn out to be right. (In the short run, the air staff was correct as it was not until later in the decade, with the introduction of the Hurricane and the Spitfire, that a fighter had the speed or climbing capacity to offer a credible defence against a bomber attack.[3]) Ironically, the focus of the early 1930s on building bombers meant that when the emphasis did shift to fighters, the latest models could be built without the air force being saddled with older planes.

Bombing increasingly became a sort of obsession in popular thinking and was one reason why so many were convinced that another war must be avoided at all costs. After Hitler's ascent to power in 1933, there was a growing sense that war with Germany was a definite possibility. Many of those on the right in Britain envisioned Germany yet again destroying the balance of power, wishing to become a dominant force in the world. Those on the left saw the Nazis as an increasing threat to civilization, a new barbarism. For practically all, war, in large part because of aerial bombing, was viewed as a terrifying alternative, bringing conflict with foreigners to home soil for the first time in centuries. (Although Britain had had plenty of experience of internecine warfare, particularly in the civil wars of the seventeenth century and when the Stuarts had tried to reclaim their throne by force of arms in the eighteenth, it was commonly if erroneously believed that no foreigners had invaded the country since the Normans in 1066. But such incursions had been comparatively minor: the troops who came with William III in 1688 and the few French who had landed in Ireland in 1798.)

In pre-modern warfare, civilians had been far from safe, with noncombatant deaths common. The bomber now meant that civilians were yet again at serious risk on a far wider scale than ever before. Even before the First World War, this fear was richly fed by literature, most prominently by H. G. Wells's 1898 novel

The War of the Worlds.[4] Although this book told the story of an invasion from Mars, the sort of destruction and panic it induced resonated with readers between the wars as they worried about bombing attacks. In 1908 Wells published *The War in the Air* which depicted the destruction of New York City by German bombers.[5] In 1933, Wells added more anxiety to the public's fear of bombing attacks with *The Shape of Things to Come*, which was soon made into a popular movie, *Things to Come*, in 1936. This later novel had a similar message, focusing on the destruction of civilization and the rise of warlords. Even though the book ended in a scientific utopia, its prediction of the panic and destruction that would happen on the way to that conclusion was devastating. Bertrand Russell wrote in 1936 that when London was bombed it would be "one vast raving bedlam, the hospitals will be stormed, traffic will cease, the homeless will shriek for help, the city will be a pandemonium."[6]

Another popular novel, *The Gas War of London*, published in 1931 by "Miles," included such passages as "In the dark streets the burned and wounded, bewildered and panic-stricken, fought and struggled like beasts, scrambling over the dead and dying alike, until they fell and were in turn trodden underfoot by the ever-increasing multitude about them."[7] As Constantine FitzGibbon vividly wrote in his 1957 study of the Blitz, even the disposal of bodies would present a problem: "With the city on fire above-ground, the few roads still open crowded with hysterical refugees, and the tubes crammed with starving, panic-stricken masses prey to virulent epidemics, it is hard to see how the corpses could even be conveyed to the pits."[8]

Civil defence did receive some attention in the 1930s. Quite early in the decade, the government started to shape its civil defence plans, concentrating on air raid wardens as well as on other aspects of civil defence. It devoted some attention to how to cope with war's effects on civilians. It drew on its experience of the General Strike of 1926 and adopted a similar scheme of regional commissioners to deal with problems in designated parts of the country. However, in many ways the General Strike system was an unfortunate precedent, in its implication of an unruly population that needed to be controlled. At the time of the General Strike, young men of the middle and upper classes had become special constables. Air raid wardens might be similar and the effort might be volunteer and amateur – people doing their bit. But such a system to some reflected a patronizing and indeed possibly distrustful attitude toward the working class.

An air raid warden scheme was discussed as early as 1934, patterned, ironically enough, on a system of "House Wardens" instituted in Nazi Germany. In March 1936 Parliament established an Air Raid Wardens Service; at the same time an Auxiliary Fire Service came into being. The plan was launched in early 1937, but the government did not give it much prominence until the following year. With the emphasis on volunteerism, it was likely to be a largely amateur and middle-class effort, with a possible result of a tired group of individuals doing such stressful work in addition to their regular jobs.

The service was also meant to draw upon local people who presumably would be working class in working-class neighbourhoods. Most would be unpaid part-time workers, while a few would be full-time, both as wardens and as firefighters.[9] The official memorandum stated, in rather cosy terms: "The general idea of an air raid warden is that he should be a responsible member of the public chosen to be a leader and adviser of his neighbours in a small area, a street or a small group of streets, in which he is known and respected."[10] In theory it all sounded quite calm, with each civil defence post in charge of about 500 residents, its several local wardens directing people to shelters, supporting morale, and reporting where bombs had fallen. Local people would know the neighbourhoods, but when raids actually started they might be themselves distracted from their tasks through losing their own houses or indeed having relatives killed or wounded. In some more radical areas in London, such as Poplar, wardens were elected.[11]

It was assumed that they would be individuals over 30, and women might be recruited as well. Although some might be paid, the system was based on the tradition of generally unpaid volunteerism. The authorities hoped to recruit about 250,000 to 300,000 participants.[12] At this point the planning was based on the quite terrifying idea – ultimately totally erroneous – that heavy raids might result in 200,000 casualties per week, of whom 66,000 would be killed. (This was approximately the total number of British civilians killed by bombing during the entire war.) This was based on the calculation – again quite wrong – that 600 tons of bombs would be dropped each day.[13] In fact the total load of bombs dropped on London during the entire war was 18,000 tons.[14] These calculations were not arbitrary but were based on the best estimates by scientific and military experts. Nevertheless, they fortunately turned out to be wrong.

Government consultations with local authorities over the air raid warden plan began in the summer of 1937, but not much happened until the following summer. By the end of June 1938, however, almost 500,000 people had been recruited nationwide. But for London, where the government wanted 100,000 volunteers, only 40,000 had joined up.[15] In total, 200,000 London wardens served, but only 16,000 of these were full-time; the latter were paid the princely sum of 3 pounds a week.[16] During the war, the warden system would become both more centralized and less voluntary. Trained wardens were being lost to the armed services but gradually compromises were worked out so that the younger men went into military service while the older trained wardens remained.

At the very bottom of the system were units of three to six wardens, each responsible for approximately 500 people. Their tasks were to issue gas masks, enforce the blackout, urge people to take shelter, and generally assist the public before, during, and after air raids. They would also telephone to a control centre to request rescue units, mostly to dig out people buried under buildings, as well as stretcher parties and firemen. In practice, telephone service frequently broke down, and boy messengers on bicycles filled the gap. Wardens might do some preliminary firefighting as well, helping to put out small blazes.

In 1938, a government-issued training pamphlet suggested, "In time of war, an air-raid warden should regard himself, first and foremost, as a member of the public chosen and trained to be a leader of his fellow-citizens and, with them and for them, do the right thing in an emergency."[17] What was the right thing was not spelled out, perhaps because the government did not want to alarm the public. Instead, most pre-war warnings – perhaps still affected by the memories of gas warfare in the First World War – primarily involved preparations for dealing with gas attacks.

For purposes of civil defence, Britain was divided into nine regions. The London region consisted of Greater London and parts of five neighbouring counties: from Tilbury to Windsor, Biggin Hill to St Albans. There were 95 separate authorities to be coordinated. The area comprised about 9 million people, although as many as 2 million left at some point during the Blitz. Sir John Anderson, at this point in the Cabinet as Home Secretary and Minister for Home Security, was appointed the Regional Commissioner for London. He asked Sir Harold Scott, a longtime civil servant, to be in charge of London, with the grand title of the Chief Administrative Officer of the London Region. In the press he became known as the "Dictator of London." The system was placed on high alert on August 23, 1939, and by September 3, the control centre, or Headquarters, was established at the Geological Museum on Exhibition Road in Kensington. During the period of the Phoney War in Britain from September 1939 to August 1940 there was little for the wardens to do, and their numbers were scaled back.[18] In London, there were at this point 9,000 paid, full-time wardens, 10,000 stretcher bearers, and 12,000 rescue workers.[19]

As such preparations testify, the common assumption that the British government did not prepare for war and was not aware of the threat is certainly not true. From 1934 on, the British government based its planning on the assumption that Germany would be the enemy. Preparations were being made, but they were far from adequate. The political opposition, the Labour Party, had a tendency to think that rearmament itself might well increase the possibility of war. Winston Churchill was the strongest voice for preparing for war, but he had in other ways made himself a political maverick, particularly in his absolute opposition to India moving toward self-government.

In terms of the war from the air, the government had decided that poison gas was very likely to be used. Gas had been effectively employed in the First World War and had left a bitter and terrifying memory. The Italians used gas in the Abyssinian war. By the time of the outbreak of war on September 3, 1939, practically everyone had a gas mask (38 million had been distributed). It may be true that British preparedness forestalled any such gas attacks.

The government issued memoranda on such topics as the treatment of casualties and the organization of air raid preparations, but such steps were taken in the context of an administration that hoped for peace through appeasement. The central authorities were making suggestions to local authorities, but the national government was only willing to pay a small part of the projected expense. Britain had not recovered from the Depression, and localities were not inclined to spend money on preparations for a war that might not happen. In any case, the mechanics of local government were not geared to make plans for wartime. Whether controlled by the left or right, local authorities did not pursue steps energetically. The descendant of the Poor Law Authorities, the Unemployment Assistance Board on the central level and Public Assistance Committees on the local, were turned to as the potential agencies to deal with those made homeless by bombing. Their long tradition of patronizing the poor was unlikely to make them an effective agency for such action. These agencies were designed to deal with destitution, a quite different situation, particularly psychologically, from that in which the bombed-out were likely to find themselves.

Early on, despite making some preparations, the government had taken the decision, for better or worse, to try not to alarm the public. As T. H. O'Brien wrote in the official history of civil defence, "Should the public be told beforehand in the interests of national safety of a threat that might never materialise? Or should the risk of maintaining secrecy be taken, in the hope that if the worst did happen the necessary courage and steadfastness would be forthcoming?"[20] The government, despite its limited faith in the people's resolve, opted for the second course, although gradually it alerted local authorities to the possible dangers that became increasingly clear to anyone who read the newspapers.

"But until war actually occurred, the education of the public in this matter should only, the [Government Air Raid Preparation] committee concluded, be slow, gradual and deliberate." At the same time the ARP committee had ended its 1925 report some years before with a dependence on British national character. "It has been borne in upon us that in the next war it may well be that that nation, whose people can endure aerial bombardment the longer and with the greater stoicism, will ultimately prove victorious."[21] The government and its civil servants had a doubly paradoxical attitude toward its population. Essentially the population was not trusted with knowing how serious the threat of war and the consequences of bombing might be, but when and if war actually broke out, it was hoped that everyone would nevertheless react well. At the same time many at the governing level had limited confidence that the majority of the population would actually do so.

The German occupation of Austria in March 1938 was a further indication that war might be coming. The bombing of Barcelona by Franco's forces in Spain that same month made even more apparent the danger of air raids. The beginning of the Czech crisis over the Sudetenland in May increased the sense of anxiety. Preparations were beset by a certain schizophrenia that hampered efforts. On the one hand the dangers were apparent. On the other, perhaps if they weren't paid much attention to they would go away. Progress was slow, as the central authorities didn't press hard, and in any case the local authorities were slow to respond.

It was hardly surprising that so many greeted with such enthusiasm and relief the Munich agreement that September between Germany, France and Britain. It was designed to prevent war through the sacrifice of the Sudetenland to Germany. Perhaps Hitler would be satisfied and war would not take place. Neville Chamberlain called it "Peace with honour" and "Peace in our time," terms rapturously received at the time, but that were bitterly ironic a year later when war broke out. A further irony, of course, was that the Munich agreement led many to realize that war was more likely to happen rather than less and increased the commitment to attempting to prepare for it.

In planning how to handle a war on the home front, the powers that be had little faith in the morale of the people. As in Wells's novels, there was an expectation that there would be intense panic. For example, the government opposed the tube stations being used as shelters because it feared that Londoners getting together would communicate panic to one another and develop a defeatist "shelter-mentality." (The tube shelters did eventually become a dramatic part of the Blitz, but at most only 177,000 people a night sought refuge in them.)

Instead, as a practical measure and also perhaps to prevent people from congregating underground, the government started to distribute so-called Anderson shelters. Each consisted of 14 pieces of corrugated steel, six girders, nuts and bolts and a spanner (wrench) to assemble the shelter. It was then shaped into a small hut that, installed in the garden, was a very effective protection for all but a direct hit. But they were expensive. Of the 15,000 distributed in the East Ham district in London, prices ranged according to size, from 6 pounds 14 shillings to 10 pounds 8 shillings, payable in instalments. It was rather grandly pointed out that the shelters were exempt from rates (real estate taxes)![22] But those who earned less than 250 pounds a year could have a shelter without charge. Assembled, the standard Anderson shelter (for six persons) was 6 feet high, 4½ feet wide and 6½ feet long; and it was meant to be buried to a depth of 3 or 4 feet, and to be covered with at least 15 inches of soil. Because of these requirements, those with private

2. Distributed by the Government, Anderson shelters suited those with at least some garden space. Mrs Beaumont of 11 Trentham Street, Southfields disguised the corrugated iron roof of her shelter as a rockery.

gardens would end up as the principal beneficiaries of the 2.25 million shelters that were distributed.[23] Andersons could be damp, were prone to flooding, and were crowded and depressing. And they were designed for very short stays, so they became quite uncomfortable for the long-time shelter they ended up providing.

In his government's dealings with Hitler, Chamberlain drew the line at Germany's invasion of Poland. As a result of Germany's doing so, at 11 a.m. on September 3, 1939, Britain and Germany were at war. At 11:27, London heard for the first time the two-minute wail of the air-raid siren, the "howl of the banshee," but it turned out to be a false alarm. A government publication of 1942 with the emblematic title of *Front Line* tells us that the first German bomb to fall on Britain in the Second World War was on October 17, 1939, on Hoy in the Orkneys.

The next nine months were something of a false alarm themselves, known as the Phoney War, although a British civilian was killed by a raid on March 16, 1940, in the Orkneys, where the Germans were presumably after naval bases. The war recommenced in April 1940, when the Germans conquered most of Western Europe. One after another, Denmark, Norway, the Low Countries and France fell. The most disastrous occasion for the British was the defeat at Dunkirk. Ironically, this evacuation became an emblematic event, almost seen as a victory, as 338,226 troops including 125,000 French troops were ferried across the Channel from Dunkirk to England between May 28 and June 4 in all sorts of ships: it was regarded as a triumph over adversity, despite the fact that 30,000 British troops were left behind (not to mention virtually all equipment) to become prisoners of war.[24]

Many in Britain took a perverse pleasure in their now isolated situation. Their attitude was "Very well, alone," or to put it another way, "Thank God, alone." (Of course, virtually all recognized how parlous the situation was, being the only European power left opposing the Nazis, and many would have preferred to have surviving allies!) Winston Churchill himself remarked, "We now stand all alone against the embattled might of Germany." The Prime Minister, who had taken office less than three weeks before

Dunkirk, went on: "And I for one, find it most inspiring."[25] (It is far too easy to either exaggerate Churchill's accomplishments or not to give him sufficient credit. He was not trusted by many on both the left and the right. Yet Churchill's speeches were increasingly listened to; as he said himself, he was privileged to give the "roar" of the lion, his aim was victory, "at all costs, victory in spite of all terror.")

In the September 7, 1940 issue of the *Times Literary Supplement*, Dorothy L. Sayers published a poem called "The English War." She took the "alone" position quite seriously, seemingly not even including the Welsh and Scots.

Praise God, now, for an English war –
    The grey tide and the sullen coast,
The menace of the urgent hour,
The single island, like a tower,
    Ringed with an angry host.

This is the war that England knows,
    When all the world holds but one man –
King Philip of the galleons,
Louis, whose light outshone the sun's,
    The conquering Corsican;

When Europe, like a prison door,
    Clangs; and the swift, enfranchised sea
Runs narrower than a village brook;
And men who love us not, yet look
    To us for liberty;

When no allies are left, no help
    To count upon from alien hands,
No waverers remain to woo,
No more advice to listen to,
    And only England stands. ...[26]

Even before Dunkirk and the French armistice with the Nazis, signed on June 22, the war in Britain escalated to a new level of intensity with the bombing of the country that spring. The first bombs on the mainland fell on Canterbury on May 9, 1940 and the first industrial town bombed was Middlesbrough, on May 24. The first bombs in the London area fell on June 18, and the first daylight attacks, with notable fatalities, were on July 1 on Wick and Hull.[27]

Nevertheless, even during wartime, life in the capital proved quite pleasant, as Virginia Cowles, an American reporter, observed. Describing London in the summer of 1940, she wrote: "Life was more informal than it had ever been before – you even saw women strolling down Bond Street in slacks and sweaters, sometimes complete with picture hat and Pekinese. People ... went to cinemas, football matches and races. Occasionally the sirens sounded, but only a few raiders penetrated ... during the summer and people seldom bothered to take cover."[28]

Britain was essentially alone in Europe, although she was supported by her Empire and Commonwealth. The United States, though neutral and far away, sent military supplies to Britain, including 50 destroyers transferred in return for the lease of military bases in the British West Indies and Newfoundland. Hitler was now in a position to turn his attention to the conquest and the invasion of Britain. He also thought Britain would appreciate the hopelessness of the situation and would be interested in negotiating a peace. In theory Hitler was willing to make terms – he would leave Britain its Empire and in return, Britain would leave Europe to Germany. But Hitler was not trusted and even what he might allegedly offer would not be acceptable.

Hitler had hoped that Britain would sue for peace; he had, after all, conquered virtually all of Europe. He had put out an unsuccessful peace feeler on July 19, then decided on August 1 to bomb Britain into submission, through attacks on air bases, aeroplane factories and harbours. He reserved to himself the right to order terror raids. (He would claim that he never did so and that he was only attacking military targets even in London, that his bombers were under orders to bring back their bombs if they did not find their designated destinations. He contended that it was the British who were terror bombing Berlin. And indeed, with a great deal of justification, the Allies would later in the war be accused of terror bombing Germany and Japan.)

The next stage of the war was the Battle of Britain. Hitler felt he needed air superiority before an invasion of Britain could be launched, and it was to that task that he turned his attention. Hitler could now use France as a base and send his aeroplanes on the short flight across the English Channel. He could also use the Channel ports to build up his invasion fleet, but he needed to eliminate the power of the British air force. On August 8, 1940 the German Luftwaffe began the bombing of British ports and harbours, and it expanded to targeting airfields on August 12 and factories soon afterward. Bombs fell as far north as Scotland, various suburbs of London were sporadically hit, and a number of bombs even fell on central London. "The few" (as the fighter pilots of the Royal Air Force were referred to) were stretched to their limits. Although the new technology dubbed radar was not fully functioning yet, it provided some help in tracking German planes. As a result, the RAF could wait to take to the skies until German bombers and fighters were near, rather than being up in the air looking for planes. As landing strips were bombed, the RAF's ability to get its fighters up in the air was severely hampered. German troops might have invaded England, as they did elsewhere, by parachute, but Hitler was also considering an invasion by sea. Though he had been wavering, he became most convinced of its possibility at the end of August, when he thought air superiority was about to be achieved. Hitler's decision not to invade might have cost him victory. But he was strategically right that it would be an extremely high risk if Germany did not possess air superiority.

The Luftwaffe had twice as many aircraft as the RAF, but with characteristic incisiveness, the historian A. J. P. Taylor has observed that this was not quite as dire for the British as one might think:

> Bombers could operate successfully only if secure from attacks by fighters, and in fighter aircraft the two opposing forces were about equal. … The British were operating on their home ground, the German fighters at the limit of their range. … Above all, the British knew what they were doing; the Germans did not. The German air chiefs never made up their minds whether the Luftwaffe should proceed with bombing, regardless of fighter attacks, or whether it should destroy the British fighters first. … In direct fighter comparisons, the British lost more than the Germans. This was eclipsed by the enormous losses in German bombers.[29]

But also the Germans were surprisingly ill-equipped, even though they had so many planes. Their bombers didn't have enough range, they couldn't carry enough bombs, and they didn't have enough defensive armour; their fighters, primarily Messerschmitts, could not operate effectively as they were ordered to slow their pace in order to stay close to the bombers. Fortunately, radar and the breaking of the German codes also helped the British.[30]

On August 15, 62 people were killed in a raid on Croydon, a London suburb with an important air base; in the weeks to follow, Wimbledon, Richmond, Dulwich and, a little further out, Slough, were also hit. In the days before September 7, the Germans also bombed Bristol, Birmingham, and Liverpool.

Only in retrospect did the heavy bombing that started on September 7 make the earlier attacks seem less important. Those raids did not have the concentrated impact of the bombing and deaths day after day that began on September 7, although they certainly were vastly unpleasant for the people who experienced them. For instance, for the earlier period, Mrs M. Stevenson, who lived in Enfield, an outlying district of London, recorded in her diary the raids that took place before September 7: "[August 22] Air raid at 3:30 am. [August 25] Two raids. [August 26] Bad raid – 5 bombs at Enfield west 6 hours. [August 28] Bad raid 7 hrs. [August 31] 6 Raids!! [September 1] Raids. [September 2] Raids. [September 3] 2 daytime raids. One short evening raid."[31]

Even before September 7 there had been a notable number of British civilian deaths by bombing – 258 in July and 1,078 in August, including 136 children and 393 women.[32] On August 31, when the first bombs fell on Kensington, the war came nearer to the centre of London. Even so, the attacks on civilian targets were still considered "nuisance" raids and did not have the impact of a concentrated bombing of the metropolis. Mrs M. (Molly) Fenlon wrote in her diary that she "expected something big from about the middle of August. The air raid warning – that stomach-turning banshee wail." But then, when it actually happened, she wrote: "On

Saturday 7th September, the 'fun' began, and it was one of those clear golden days. ... [I] was surprised to find that I was not as frightened as I thought I would be."[33]

Before September 7, the bombing might be serious but it wasn't taken all that seriously. In a manuscript in the Imperial War Museum entitled "Journal under the Terror," Miss P. Warner wrote about her experiences on Sunday, September 1. She had just been to a jolly Fabian Summer School in Devon. "We dance and bathe and play and argue as if there were no air-raid warnings and thuds of guns and dull explosions, no daily score of brave young airmen who have lost their lives." Back in London on Tuesday she found it "apparently unchanged in spite of the frequent air-raid warnings. Familiarity has bred contempt, and the heart-chilling wail of the siren has been followed so often by a deathly silence that it now means little. The streets remain crowded, lovers wander arm-in-arm, children play their games, men tend their gardens undisturbed."

On Friday, September 6, despite there being a raid, she had a day of pleasure little affected by any bombs. "Today I attended a Promenade Concert at the Queens Hall. ... It was a Beethoven concert, and although the warning had gone, the entire hall was packed with a mammoth audience. On to a theatre where a further warning had no effect on a big audience, and then to a restaurant jam-packed with jovial beings and home through streets whizzing with traffic under an impressive display of searchlights."[34] There would be a dramatic change the next day. As another diarist wrote about the period from Saturday, August 31, to Thursday, September 5: "Warning after warning. Wail after wail. Siren after siren but never any activity. London may yet escape the fury of the attacking German Luftwaffe."

London's citizens were becoming increasingly vulnerable. On August 24, contrary to Hitler's orders and to his fury, two German bombers let their bombs go over London. In retaliation, Churchill ordered 81 British bombers to attack Berlin. These British raids caused minimal damage and were essentially quite ineffective, but they were a deeply embarrassing refutation of the pledge by Hermann Goering, the head of the Luftwaffe, that no enemy bomber would fly over Germany. On September 3, Goering met with Field Marshals Kesselring and Sperrle to press his view that now London itself should be bombed. He believed that the British air force had been sufficiently weakened to make this possible; Kesselring agreed, Sperrle did not.[35] Kesselring thought bombing London would in fact deliver the final blow to the RAF, and that it would also destroy London's docks and factories. By Germany's attacking the great imperial city, the British might be driven to sue for peace without an invasion.

At a huge rally in Berlin on September 4, Hitler promised an imminent invasion and to raze London to the ground. (The next day, with characteristic British practicality, Churchill rose in the House of Commons to pledge that there would be compensation for bomb damage.) That night, September 4, Hitler gave Goering permission to bomb London systematically. However, as A. J. P. Taylor has pointed out, there may well have been a difference of opinion between Hitler and Goering. Hitler hoped for a negotiated peace but he also had been moving forward with his invasion plan, Operation Sea Lion. He may have thought that the British would be more likely to negotiate a peace if London were not heavily bombed. Goering, as head of the air force, wished to defeat Britain through air power. He might have done so if he had been a better commander. He insisted that the German fighter planes stick near the bombers, not allowing them to use their skills of speed, climbing and diving. The British were much more in command of the situation than it might appear, given their apparent desperate plight and their resources being so stretched. According to Taylor, the Germans lost 1,733 aircraft during the Battle of Britain, while the British lost 915.[36] From July 10 until October 31, 1940 the Royal Air Force battled German aircraft over Britain. Germany inflicted devastating raids on Britain, but these were never as devastating as the Germans hoped.[37]

Bombing was very inexact. And those who bombed knew it. The Germans could claim, with some legitimacy, that they were bombing military targets. In the first few weeks of the Battle of Britain, the Germans did indeed target military sites – airfields and factories and harbours. Despite the extent of their bombing, however, there was amazingly little damage to the factories producing the matériel the British needed. Nor did the raids actually interrupt the pace of military production too much; that was largely because of a system of having spotters on the roofs of factories so that workers did not take shelter when the sirens sounded but rather only once the planes were seen nearly overhead.

Hitler claimed he was not employing terror bombing, although he was aware and hoped that his bombing might be terrifying. Before September 7, a few German raids hit other suburbs besides Croydon and some bombs fell on more central parts of London. Many of these so-called nuisance raids took place during daylight. But the price the Germans were paying was becoming too high, as daylight made it easier for British fighters to destroy German bombers. The Germans had failed to eliminate the Royal Air Force, and they had failed to cripple war production. Nor did the bombing appear to have weakened morale. Now Hitler would discover if he could possibly do all three through the mass bombing of London. He announced that he would reduce London to rubble – inevitably (although he would deny it), terror would be part of the operation.

III

September 7, 1940

"Everything looked liked fairyland"

THE GERMANS selected September 7 to start the Blitz, a day that soon came to be called "Black Saturday."[1] It was the largest single bombing raid ever up to that point. Not only was the extent of the bombing that first day unprecedented, but the London Blitz would continue longer than any other series of air raids. It would last until May 10, 1941. September 7 heralded the worst period with bombing on 56 out of 57 consecutive nights, with one night's reprieve due to cloudy skies. During that period, London was bombed, and bombed heavily, every night by an average of 200 bombers.[2] Other British cities were attacked with devastating effect, but no other city was bombed day in and day out.

September 7 was a beautiful day, and uncharacteristically for London at the time of year, the temperature was in the nineties. Although everyone knew in theory that a heavy raid might take place any day, there was no awareness that there would be a seismic shift in the course of the war that day. That change is suggested by a comment Mary Eleanor (known as Mea) Allan, a reporter and novelist, made on September 9 in a letter: "You felt you really were walking with death – death in front of you & death hovering in the skies."[3]

The Germans had begun preparing for some military action – whether an invasion or not was unclear – during the preceding week. The number of barges the Germans gathered at Ostend had grown from 18 to 270. All German army leave had been stopped. The full moon between September 8 and 10 would be particularly favourable. Hermann Goering, the chief of the Luftwaffe, travelled from Berlin to Normandy for the first wave of air attacks. On the afternoon of September 7, he stationed himself at Cap Gris Nez and trained his binoculars on the white cliffs of Dover, a mere 22 miles away. That day Goering rather bombastically stated on the radio:

> As a result of the provocative British attacks on Berlin on recent nights, the Führer had decided to order a mighty blow to be struck in revenge against the capital of the British Empire. I personally have assumed the leadership of the attack, and today I have heard above me the roaring of the victorious German squadrons which now, for the first time, are driving towards the heart of the enemy in full daylight, accompanied by countless fighter squadrons. ... This is an historic hour, in which for the first time the German Luftwaffe has struck at the heart of the enemy.[4]

The bombers were scheduled to release their loads over London after 5 o'clock in the afternoon. The waves of German planes, miles long, both bombers and fighters, were formidable and terrifying. Their presence, the noise, the destruction, the fires, the deaths, the injuries, the chaos would, it was thought, bring Britain to its knees. London, hitherto only lightly bombed, and that mostly on the outskirts, would be destroyed by incendiaries and high explosives.

In retrospect, the beautiful and unseasonably warm Saturday was at first ominously quiet. Other than a few German reconnaissance aircraft, no German bombers or fighter planes were spotted until late afternoon, when radar stations in the southeast noted planes taking off from the Pas de Calais. The 348 German bombers and 617 Messerschmitt German fighters formed a terrifying sight. The British Hurricane and Spitfire fighters were caught off guard.

At 4:14 p.m. the German bombers and fighters crossed the coast into England. When the planes first appeared, the spotters assumed that they would split up and head for their customary targets – air bases, factories, and the gas tanks on the outskirts of London – rather than continuing en masse to the capital.

That afternoon, Virginia Cowles, the American journalist, had gone into the countryside to visit friends at Mereworth Castle, a splendid eighteenth-century Palladian-style villa in Kent. In the late afternoon they were enjoying tea on the lawn.

> Suddenly we heard the drone of planes. At first we couldn't see anything, but soon the noise had grown into a deep, full roar, like the far-away thunder of a giant waterfall. We lay in the grass, our eyes strained towards the sky; we made out a batch of tiny white specks, like clouds of insects, moving north-west in the direction of the capital. Some of them – the bombers – were flying in even formation, while the others – the fighters – swarmed protectively around.[5]

Harold Nicolson, author, former diplomat, Member of Parliament, husband of Vita Sackville-West, and currently working in the Ministry of Information, observed the raid at their country house, Sissinghurst, in Kent, from the great garden he and his wife had created together. The English weekend, particularly for those of a certain class, went on. On his way down earlier in the day, at Tonbridge station, he had observed two very young captured German airmen. "One of them just looks broken down and saturnine; the other had a superior half-smile on his face, as if thinking, 'My Führer will pay them out for this.' The people on the platform are extraordinarily decent. They just glance at them and then turn their heads away, not wishing to stare." Later, he and Vita were sitting outside. "We have tea and watch the Germans coming over in wave after wave. There is some fighting above our heads and we hear one or two aeroplanes zoom downwards. They flash like silver gnats above us in the air."[6]

By 4:30 p.m. 21 British fighter squadrons were or were about to be in the air. "'I'd never seen so many aircraft,' wrote Squadron Leader Sandy Johnstone of 602 Squadron. 'It was a hazy sort of day to about 16,000 feet. As we broke through the haze, you could

3. When the first sirens sounded, many Londoners were reluctant to spoil their afternoon and take shelter. Edward Ardizzone, *The Trek to the Shelters, Silvertown, September 1940.*

hardly believe it. As far as you could see, there was nothing but German aircraft coming in, wave after wave.'"[7]

The air-raid sirens went off in London at 4:43 p.m. As the German planes neared the capital, the day was so idyllic that it made some residents reluctant to take shelter when they first heard the sirens. Miss Mott, for instance, wrote in her diary: "The zooming of planes spoils the lovely air which is so pleasant that it is a shame to go in, *as one ought*."[8]

When the planes were first heard, many thought they were British aircraft – until the bombs actually began to fall. Len Jones, an 18-year-old in Poplar, a poor district in London targeted because of its warehouses and gasworks, remembered his reactions.

> That afternoon, around five o'clock, I went outside the house. I'd heard the aircraft, and it was very exciting, because the first formations were coming over without any bombs dropping, but very, very majestic; terrific. And I had no thought that they were actually bombers. Then from that point on I was well aware, because bombs began to fall, and shrapnel was going along King Street, dancing off the cobbles. Then the real impetus came, in so far as the suction and the compression from the high explosive blasts just pulled you and pushed you, and the whole of this atmosphere was turbulating so hard that, after an explosion of a nearby bomb, you could actually feel your eyeballs being sucked out. I was holding my eyes to try and stop them going. And the suction was so vast, it ripped my shirt away, and ripped my trousers. Then I couldn't get my breath, the smoke was like acid and everything round me was black and yellow. And these bombers just kept on and on, the whole road was moving, rising and falling.[9]

One Londoner, Viola Bawtree, was fairly calm as the German planes approached.

> Elaine had just put pastry in the oven, it seemed such a mistake to turn off gas so we all hung about listening, with only Mrs P. & baby down in cellar. Kenneth & Mr P. put on shrapnel helmets & stood out looking up. S. put the kettle on & made tea, & we sat in dining room & had it. The first time we stayed up since sirens started. I hope we keep to it. Then Kenneth went to look again, & when he called out there was a whole crowd of Jerrys approaching we thought we'd feel safer down in the cellar. . . . All clear about 6.30. I ran Tigger over the field then hurried to have a bath.[10]

Jack Graham Wright, at the time an architectural student living at home in Plumstead in southeast London, wrote about his experience in 1997. His family did not believe that serious raids would happen and hence did not have a shelter. In the Wright house the beginning of the first heavy raid was marked, as it was all over London, by tea. "It must have been about four o'clock, because my mother had made afternoon tea for the three of us [his brother and himself], when the air-raid warning sirens sounded. She brought in the little silver-edged tray, complete with cups and saucers, a small, matching china jug with milk, and a teapot under its cosy." He and his mother went to look out and saw the massed German planes. His mother asked, "'What are all those little bright things underneath them?'" Then they both realized that they were bombs and decided to retreat into the cupboard under the stairs.

> We all became conscious of a growing crescendo of noise drowning the growl of the planes, and then a series of enormous

> thuds growing nearer. These were making the ground to heave so that we could feel through our bodies the shocks coming up from under the boards of the floor, which jerked and moved strangely. I leaned on the door-jamb to steady myself, when the biggest crunch of all came with the hugest noise. The air of the parlour condensed and became opaque as if turned instantaneously to a red-brown fog, the floor heaved unbelievably, the party-wall (that solid safe brick wall) leaned and rocked as though it had become flexible and my door-post moved with such determination that I almost lost my balance and toppled against my mother. All at the same time as these writhings the slates from the roof came pouring down, crashing through the roof of the glass conservatory with huge clatter, smashing all the glass and piling brokenly into the room. I could hear doors and windows crashing all over the place, as the heaving subsided and we realised that the wall had stopped moving without collapsing. ... The brown fog had gone, but everything was covered with a heavy brown dust, which lay so thickly on the floor that it concealed the carpet. The little china milk jug was lying on its side, and the spilt milk lay in a rivulet dripping over the edge of the table to a white pool in that thick layer of dust below. My mother made an instinctive movement to pick up the jug and staunch the flow of milk, but realised how useless it was. What normally would have been a serious accident spoiling the carpet, was tiny in this new scale of destruction.

A bomb had left a huge crater in the garden and Jack climbed up to see over its rim. "Beyond, there was a chaos of nothingness. An ugly conical crater extended between our house and the shattered houses of the terrace whose gardens backed to ours."[11]

Also in southeast London, the Rev. B. P. Mohan, the vicar of St John's, Penge, did not have much sense of the need to take shelter. Instead, he spent most of his time fulfilling his parochial duties.

> There was terrific bombing over [the] Thames & great clouds of smoke soon came rising up. There were countless "dog-fights" & we heard & saw fights directly overhead & a great deal of ack-ack fire. Shortly after, another very big formation of bombers & fighters came over from about SE & passed directly overhead. It seemed well over 50 machines. They started to bomb directly overhead & we heard the whistle of bombs & fell over one another in rushing into the Parochial Hall. Out we tumbled again to have a look & just in time to see a bomb explode just the other side of St. John's Church. After a short time of prayer I went out as I was convinced it was Newlands Park [a street] & found that Mrs. Moynagh's Nursing Home was struck. I walked into the undamaged part of the house & talked to the old people & invalids. They were all as calm & cool as cucumbers. ... I gathered that one old invalid man was buried under the debris & two others were injured.[12]

Years later, a man who had been 12 years old on September 7 recalled, "As we watched we could see their bomb-racks opening and bombs beginning to fall. ... My brother was at work in the Siemens factory at Charlton and my mother was very concerned for his safety. She kept saying 'If we are to be killed at least we should all be killed together.'"[13]

For some youngsters, the first raid was just another new experience, something appreciated mostly for its thrilling aspects and novelty. Bryan Forbes, the future movie director, then 13, was appropriately at a cinema. He had been evacuated from West Ham at the beginning of the war until spring 1940, and he would be sent away again after the Blitz began. But on September 7 he was inside the Odeon Theatre in Forest Gate, watching the matinee showing of *Gaslight*.[14]

> Halfway through the performance the audience became conscious of what seemed to be a hail storm beating on the roof. The projector lamp died and the house lights came up. The limp manager, in black tie, came on to the stage and announced that the audience should disperse in the interests of safety. We trooped without undue haste into the bright sunshine outside and stood in groups on the pavement watching pattern after pattern of sun-silvered Dorniers winging high overhead.

He then went home and for two days and nights lived in the family's Anderson shelter. "I felt curiously, irrationally secure in the fetid darkness of the small shelter."[15]

Nineteen-year-old Leslie Jerman, later a journalist for *The Scotsman*, also found the beginning of the Blitz rather exciting as he remembered it all 50 years later. He was then living with his large family in East Ham. "I had never before seen such a sight in my life. ... The aircraft moved slowly on. ... I could see black crosses on the wings. ... I had had no experience of air-raids and felt no fear. It was somewhat thrilling. ... Suddenly I heard an explosion. Then another and another. Soon my father came down [our road] from the High Street with the news. East Ham Station Bridge had been bombed. Woolworths store was flat."[16]

Jo Oakman kept a diary recording the raids, starting on August

17. She was an artist, the daughter of a curate, and worked in the food office in Chelsea Town Hall. She was also a warden. She made several entries on September 7, typically noting that she was having her tea when the sirens went, she recorded, at 5 p.m. Then at 5:05 she wrote about the noise rather cheerfully: "Just like a good old Guy Faulke's [sic] day."[17] When the All Clear sounded after the first raid, she was sufficiently relaxed that she decided to go to the cinema.

Barbara Nixon was a young actress who was also serving as a warden in the Finsbury section of London. She had studied English as an undergraduate at Newnham College, Cambridge and in 1931 had married, as his second wife, the Communist economist and Cambridge don Maurice Dobb. On that Saturday afternoon, as families came into the shelters, she noted, "Nobody was seriously frightened. There had been repeated 'alerts' and a few actual bombs dropped during the preceding weeks. Something might possibly happen this time, but probably not." The wardens thought a major raid would come, contrary, in her opinion, to the belief held by most Londoners. Finsbury was four miles from the docks area and soon the huge fires were clearly visible. "From our vantage-point it was remote and, from a spectacular point of view, beautiful. One had to force oneself to picture the misery and the havoc down below in the most overcrowded area of London; the panic and the horror when suddenly bombs had fallen in the busy, narrow street markets and bazaars, and on the rickety houses."[18]

There were others besides Nixon who agreed that this brief "introductory" raid, which lasted just over an hour, was no lark. Olive Lilian McNeil, 14 years old at the time, vividly remembered her experience in Poplar. The family was fortunate to have an Anderson shelter and a garden to put it in.

> I was in the backyard watching my two little brothers play … and I could hear this strange droning sound. Looking up I could see lots of planes very small and very high. I called the boys to look. We said how pretty they looked with the sun glinting on them, they looked like stars. … Suddenly everything changed, the planes that were high up started to swoop down and down and the air was filled with screaming whistling sounds. The siren was blowing and mum came running out and pushed us down the shelter. … Mum told us to lie down and she lay on top of us and she kept saying her prayers and I said "Please Jesus don't let the screaming whistlings come too close". … But the screaming whistling went on and on, and one got so close that the shelter nearly got lifted out of the ground. We all screamed. … Suddenly everything went quiet and we clung together in the blessed silence until the all clear went.

This was around 6 p.m., 15 minutes after the German bombers headed home. Olive recalled, "I was out first. By now it was getting dark. I remember standing by the shelter and looking around me, it was as though I was in a dream. The sky as far as I could see all around me was orange and pink. It glowed making everything look like fairyland."[19]

One firefighter, F. W. Hurd, vividly made clear the transition from the "nuisance" raids to something more serious.

> London has been subjected to "nuisance" raids for about a month. The warning would sound usually just after dark, and occasional planes would be heard droning over (we

soon became adept at distinguishing the peculiar rise & fall note of German engines). The object of these "raids" was, presumably, to disorganise transport and production and make things awkward in general. This latter it certainly did for us in the Fire Service. As soon as the warning went we were required to rig ourselves in full fire gear with respirator at the "Alert", and to stay rigged until the "All Clear" sounded. No joke this when the warning usually lasts from middle evening till the early hours of the morning. (This order for rigging was later rescinded it being necessary to don full gear only on leaving cover.)

On this particular day, Saturday 7th Sept 1940, the sirens had wailed their warning at about 4.30 pm. We heard planes and later a dog-fight could be discerned well away to the East. We also saw parachutes [with bombs] descending through the puffs of A.A. [anti-aircraft] smoke. "Over the Thames again" we said. (The Estuary & parts of the river-side up from there had been enduring raids for some time.) After a short time it was no longer possible to distinguish the planes at all, the sky being apparently empty except for a few scattered shell bursts. We entered our shelter (a room on the ground floor) and settled down to wait for the all clear & supper. ... We were getting a bit fed up with this sort of thing & I think a few of us (I know I did) half-hoped for "something to happen" & then felt ashamed for letting the monotony "get us down". Then suddenly it came! The alarm bell rang at 6:15. All pumps (2 heavy units and four trailer pumps) were ordered to Kingsland Rd Station.[20]

After the first All Clear, Jack Wright spotted his father bicycling home and ran towards him. "'It's all right, we're all right. It's just the house.'" As their own home had been destroyed, they decided to move to an empty house on Bostall Heath belonging to friends, and Jack carefully took his thesis with him. "I screwed my thesis report out of the dust-laden typewriter, and packed it quickly in my own case, and more urgently, I carried my portfolio with me. It was large and immensely heavy, but it contained my entire thesis design-drawings, now complete and ready for submission."

He reflected, rather poignantly, on the significance of the destruction of his family house.

> When I had left our house in haste, struggling with my portfolio, I was leaving my family home for ever. I never returned. The environment of my boyhood and youth, the happy place of our family life, had been physically obliterated. I could remember all its parts: the little lawn, the pond in the rockery; the warm brick wall; the great Lombardy poplars whose leaves would twinkle in the moonlight as I watched from my bedroom window. … All had been blocked out forever by that cataclysmic insult, as sudden as it was irreversible. It had been final in its brutality. … Out of all the packed incidents of that September afternoon, my mind's eye sees with sharp significance two actions of my parents during their confrontation with the destruction of their home. I see my mother's impulse to replace the little china milk jug on its tray and mop up its spilt milk, an intimate and instinctive gesture checked by her unavoidable recognition of the scale of the upheaval, so instantaneous as to be almost unbelievable. Separately, I see my father approaching the calamitous scene, his strained face as his distant eyes fixed on me, not able to get into earshot quickly enough, stumbling as he dismounted upon hearing my calls: "it's all right, Dad, we're all right."[21]

The greatest single objective of both German raids of September 7 was the huge expanse of docks located on the Thames in London's East End: Surrey Commercial, West India, Millwall, Royal Victoria and Albert, as well as the Woolwich Arsenal. The Woolwich area was bombed at 5:15 p.m., and the Arsenal itself as well as the Siemens works was badly damaged. At the Millwall Docks, 200 acres of timber exploded in flames. There was heavy destruction of oil storage tanks, causing great fires. John Hodsoll, the Inspector General of Air Raid Precautions, described the scene from the roof of the Home Office in Whitehall:

> Huge clouds of black smoke was [sic] billowing and spiralling up into the clear blue sky; great spurts of flame were shooting up; there was dull thud of bombs as they exploded and reverberated in the distance, and an acrid smell of burning was borne in on the wind. The docks looked as if they had been reduced to one great inferno. ... The spectacle had an almost eerie fascination, which held us spellbound and immobile.[22]

Clustered near the docks were the badly built homes of the very poor. The local housing stock suffered grave damage – thousands of residences were destroyed, with many people losing all their treasured possessions – in this densely populated district, which was also the area where London's poorer Jews lived. Some Jews felt that Hitler had particularly targeted the area for that reason, but that was unlikely.[23] The docks were legitimate military targets, but the German bombing up until September 7 had attempted to pinpoint air bases and factories. There were inevitably civilian targets that were bombed as well, but not then as a matter of German policy. The bombing of London was unrestricted, however, and Hitler's aim was inevitably also, whatever his claims might be, to terrorize the population and create such pressure that the government would have no choice but to ask for peace. Yet the German raids did not, amazingly, succeed in putting the docks out of commission.

Perhaps the hardest hit of the dock areas was Stepney. Approximately 200,000 people of various races lived there, with an average of 12 people in each flat, a figure that emphasizes not only how many people were affected but also the intense crowding in substandard housing in the dockland areas.[24] Bernard Kops, almost 13, lived in Stepney, and recorded vivid memories of September 7 in his 1963 memoir, *The World Is a Wedding*: "That day stands out like a flaming wound in my memory. Imagine a ground floor flat crowded with hysterical women, crying babies and great crashes in the sky and the whole earth shaking." But the Kops family rapidly recovered their spirits. "The men started to play cards and the women tried a little sing-song. ... Every so often twenty women's fists shook at the ceiling, cursing the explosions, Germany, Hitler. ... I sat under the table where above the men were playing cards, screwing my eyes up and covering my ears, counting the explosions. 'We're all gonna be killed, we're finished,' one of my aunts became hysterical. 'Churchill will get us through, he's a friend of the Yiddisher people.' With these words she was soothed." After the All Clear, he went outside and wandered about. He saw "flames shooting higher than the cranes along the dockside. ... Everything was chaos except the fire which was like a living monster with an insatiable appetite." He returned home, where the family was listening to Lord Haw-Haw, William Joyce, broadcasting from Germany that the Jews of London were all to be killed that night. The family concluded that "the Germans had set fire to the docks in order to have a beacon for the coming night of terror." About the next morning he remembered, "The boys of Stepney Green were scrubbing around in the debris near the clock tower for pieces of shrapnel. ... I went ... round to Redmans Road to look for some more. In front of me was a space where once had been the house of a boy I knew. Not a very close friend, just someone I played with occasionally. 'What happened?' I asked a warden. 'They all got killed.' Funny, I thought, I had seen him the day before and now he was no more."[25]

Jim Wolveridge, then a young man of 20, also provided an account of the first day of the Blitz in Stepney.

> My mother and my other sister, Mary, had gone out to buy something for tea. But we didn't get any that day. The shelter was in the crypt in the church that was across the road. I don't know that it was very safe but it was better than nothing. ... There were so many bombs that it was impossible to distinguish between one explosion and another. That was bad enough. But Lily [a friend of his sister] made it worse by having a fit of hysterics. She screamed so loudly that she rattled me a damned sight more than the bombs. ... In the end the Germans did it for us. One of their bombs fell on the big cargo boat anchored outside the shelter. The explosion had such a terrific impact that I felt I'd been hit over the head, and my eardrums had gone west. It did one good thing though, it shocked Lily into silence.

After the All Clear for the first raid "the old man and me went indoors to get our cure for all troubles, a good cup of tea. We didn't get one, the water and gas had been cut off." He returned to the crypt for the second raid. With the failure of the lights, they sang along with an accordion player, frequently the tune that became the virtual anthem of the London Blitz: "Roll Out the Barrel, We'll Have a Barrel of Fun," so contrary to what was actually happening.

"We began roaring out the songs, and the nearer the bombs fell, the louder we sang."[26]

The great West India Dock, located in a section of Poplar known as the Isle of Dogs, was also very badly hit. As one resident, David Marson, remarked, "The war for us on the Isle of Dogs really began on September 7th 1940."[27] A man who worked in a fire station there remembered,

> It was nearly teatime; those of us not on Control Room duty spent the time whilst waiting for tea on the verandah of our flat on the top floor of the Station, watching vapour trails. To get a better view we went inside and leaned out of the window looking towards Greenwich. We saw several aircraft coming towards us, low enough to be seen easily. They seemed to approach very slowly, their shapes, black against the clear sky, ominous and menacing. We closed the window and were making our way unhurriedly downstairs when suddenly aeroplane engines roared overhead and at the same time there came a tremendous rushing sound that got louder and louder until it terminated in terrific explosions. ... Reports were received that water mains were shattered, few hydrants were giving water; we were surrounded by water, but the tide was out, suction hoses could not reach water level.

This firefighter spent the rest of the raid in a shelter by the fire station. "I don't remember much of that night, except that I was so scared that all the things I had been frightened of before that night became insignificant and of no account." All he remembered when he looked at the street by the building the next day was "a woman walked by pushing a pram piled high with her possessions. There was nobody else in sight."[28]

T. H. Pointer, an air raid warden on duty at the docks, started his recollection rather calmly; it would almost appear that tea was his theme. "As the siren faded away the sound of airplanes was heard. Strolling to the door with a cup of tea in my hands, I looked round and up for the sight of them. … I dashed, cup in hand, for our dug-out, about 40–50 yards away. As I ran I considered throwing the tea away, but finished up with about half a cup. … After what seemed hours, but could only have been tens of seconds, [the bombing] stopped and we staggered out of the dug-out to behold the most awful chaos possible."[29] There were further confusions; landmines descended by parachute, and there was a fear that they were actual parachutists invading. The fires, heat, and smoke were so intense that bomb shelters at some of the docks had to be evacuated.

The raids of September 7 were a decisive break with what had happened so far; with them the war entered a new stage, and the home front became a battleground. On the Isle of Dogs, Mrs Brewster remembered, "The first Saturday was the frightening one, the first Saturday they raided. We'd had quite a lot of warnings, we got so used to nothing coming over that you didn't take no notice." Mrs Brewster's memoir is another that touches on the theme of tea – continuing to partake of their afternoon ritual provided a great sense of comfort to the British and reinforced their sang-froid.

> The warning went, and we thought, oh, it's nearly teatime, we'll make our way home. Before we could get home, they was over and we ended up in Glengall Road School, we couldn't go no further, we had to go down in the shelters there and stay there nearly all night, and when we came out, everything was surrounded with fire; they had surrounded the Island that night with fire. It was really terrifying, being

> the first time, you know, you didn't know what to expect, it was terrifying.[30]

Margaret Holmes, the wife of a vicar on the Isle of Dogs, also wrote about the first day of the London Blitz. She was with Dodger, the family dog, under the stairs in her house, while her husband, Arthur, was watching the bombs fall from the roof of his church. He concluded that it was not a particularly wise place to be when a bomb fell 100 yards away and he felt the church move, and after helping others, they both retired under the staircase. "We thought ours [bombs] had come. The crack was terrific. ... I went through to Dodger who was in his chair in the scullery. The back door had burst open too, but Dodger just shook himself and wagged his tail. The dust settled and we looked out. The street was carpeted thick with dust, bricks and glass. Arthur ran round the corner and met Firemaster Ayre who said, 'Was anyone in the church?' Arthur said, 'No, why? Has it gone?" 'Yes,' Arthur said, 'Oh dear. Unemployed.'"[31]

Bill Snellgrove, then a schoolboy, provides a vivid overview, as seen from Eltham, just south of Woolwich, of the bombing in this part of London that day. He and his best friend, Merv Haisman, who had been evacuated to the countryside, exchanged very lively letters during the two years they were separated, from the beginning of the war until September 1941, when Merv returned to London. They would appear to be rather sophisticated kids. Bill wrote on September 15, 1940 to describe his experiences on September 7.

> Surely it will become an historic date? Mum was just making tea early Saturday evening after a shopping expedition to Beresford Square. ... It was a lovely warm evening. ... We've been seeing a lot of enemy planes lately but this time

> we somehow sensed it was different. In spite of all the noise, there was a feeling of stillness, and believe it or not, a dog howled. Dad said this was a bad sign. Sure enough, when the bombers appeared there were too many to count. They flew in massed formation like we saw in the newsreels of the Spanish Civil War. Although we've had a lot of raids it was the first time I really felt the war in my guts. I felt angry. How dare they fly over my country as though they owned it.

Bill pursued the fire engines on his bike, rather daringly. "Spread out before me was the sort of sight Pepys must have seen during the Great Fire of London. The north side of the river was a mass of flames."[32]

IV

The Second Raid

"The peace was shattered"

THE FIRST RAID ended officially with the wail of the All Clear siren at 6:10 p.m. Everyone assumed the bombing for the day was over. They were wrong. What was extraordinary was the German decision to follow this initial raid immediately with another. This was virtually the last great daylight raid, to be succeeded relentlessly with nighttime raids every night, except one, for nearly two months.

The next raid started at 8:10 p.m. In the second wave, the Germans sent 318 bombers as well as accompanying fighter planes. They dropped 300 tons of high explosive bombs and thousands of smaller incendiary ones.[1] Throughout the second raid, the burning docks brilliantly illuminated London for the next wave of bombers. Now areas outside of the East End as well as the East End itself were relentlessly attacked. The fires at the docks could be seen for 30 miles. This raid lasted from 8:10 p.m. in the evening until 4:30 the next morning.

Mass Observation employed dozens of amateur note takers to record ordinary life throughout Britain. It had come into being in 1937, founded by Tom Harrisson, Charles Madge and Humphrey Jennings. Using observers, its object was to find out about ordinary

4. The blast of one bomb propelled a bus, empty of passengers, into a row of terraced houses, its radiator nestling in a second-floor window. Mornington Crescent, Camden Town, September 8, 1940.

life in Britain, based on Harrisson's experience as an anthropologist. It published a series of books, beginning that year with *May the Twelfth*, a study of what people were doing on the day of the coronation of George VI. During the war, it was employed by the Ministry of Information to help assess civilian morale.

One of its reports recorded the beginning of the second raid from an air-raid shelter in Stepney:

> There are three more tremendous crashes. Women scream and there is a drawing-together physically. ... There is a feeling of breath being held: everyone waiting for more. No more. People stir, shift their positions, make themselves more comfortable. ... Around midnight, a few people in the shelter are asleep but every time a bomb goes off, it wakes them. Several women are crying. At each explosion there is a

> burst of singing from the next shelter. ... When the all-clear goes, about 4.30 a.m. there is a groan of relief. But as soon as the first people get outside the shelter, there are screams of horror at the sight of the damage ... smashed windows and roofs everywhere. ... One man throws a fit; another is sick. Later that day, in the windowless front room of one of the shattered Smithy Street houses, a young woman sits among the remains of her possessions, crying her heart out: it is her birthday. "I'm twenty-six," she sobs, "I'm more than half to thirty! I wish I was dead!"[2]

Len Jones, the Poplar teenager thrilled but buffeted by the first raid, also moved into a public street shelter for the second raid and presented a less optimistic picture than one might expect.

> The shelter was brick and concrete built, and it was lifting and moving, rolling almost as if it was a ship in a rough sea. And the suction and the blasts coming in and out of the steel door, which was smashing backwards and forwards, bashed us around against the walls. The extent of injuries at that stage was just abrasions really, the shoulders and chest getting crushed against the wall, or across the floor. The worst part was the poor little kids; they were so scared, they were screaming and crying, clutching at their parents. The heat was colossal, the steel door was so hot you couldn't touch it. And everybody was being sick and people were carrying out their normal human needs, and the smell was terrible.[3]

Eric Sevareid, who would become one of the most eminent of news reporters, was then one of a group of American foreign correspondents in London. Their accounts of the Blitz provide a valuable slant on events. Assisting in the reporting of the war from Britain to America had a high priority among the British authorities as a crucial way of increasing American sympathy for the British cause. It was hoped that this would translate into aid and that eventually the United States would come into the war on Britain's side. Sevareid was at an inn in Tilbury, downriver from the East End on the Thames estuary, on the night of September 7. He joined others in a covered trench shelter.

> This night I understood terror as I never had before. … A woman employee of the inn … wept throughout the night into her apron and murmured over and over: "How's it going to end? How's it going to end?" I think few among us in that cave really expected to live through the night. Yet dawn did come. … The inn remained, and a tugboat was drifting easily with the tide. There was terror – but not panic. One could panic in his heart, but two together could not show it, nor a hundred in a group. They neutralize one another, and therein lies the thing that makes the British slightly different. They have laid manifold restraints upon themselves in their mutual intercourse.[4]

Human beings have the capacity to get used to almost anything. Even with the fear of invasion, the British demonstrated their ability to control their environment by making it more domestic. An anonymous letter dated September 8, 1940 makes that clear. It was written to a friend in the United States, so perhaps there was a conscious or unconscious wish to conform to the perception of British phlegm and stiff upper lip. "We had an invasion alarm last night. (Please, Censor, don't cut all this out; it is quite harmless and will be useless information to the enemy by the time it arrives.) Phil and I were at the flicks when just in the middle of the most exciting part of *The Thin Man* a message was flashed on the screen requiring all troops to return to their billets at once." After the woman and her husband hurried home,

> [Phil collected] his rifle and kit and dashed off to report at H.Q. I was just starting to wash my hair before the midnight news when the bell went and I went down to admit a very young, very solemn soldier. He announced that he had come to phone a message and stand by our phone throughout the night for further orders for his unit who were stationed in defensive positions around. I suggested that he leave his kit in the outer hall – "No, I'll not do that." He obviously considered that the safety of Britain hung on his every act. ... All night the telephone went – we have an extension and bell in the bedroom and I couldn't resist the temptation of listening in to Sapper Freer's discourses. I wish I could have taken them down in shorthand and sent the whole thing to *Punch*. ... At 7 A.M. Phil got home.[5]

The first night of this major raid was nevertheless very difficult, as so many of those who tried to cope had had comparatively little experience. The pressure was so great and there was so much to do that of necessity a great deal of improvisation occurred. This was the case at a first aid station at the Bermondsey Baths, where a woman physician, Dr Morton, remembered,

> When we were training the first-aid workers, we took a great deal of time explaining how they should be aseptic: how they should scrub their hands before touching any wounds, how they should take care of asepsis when putting dressings on.

> But the very first night of the Blitz that just went by the wind. What struck one was the tremendous amount of dirt and dust, the dirt and dust of ages blown up in every incident. ... Their heads were full of grit and dust, their skin was engrained with dust, and it was completely impossible to do anything much about antisepsis at all. ... Some of the bath attendants were using hose pipes to wash the people down. ... All our knowledge of what to expect was taken from various books, mainly about what had happened in Spain. And I think it was a surprise to all of us, when the first Blitz did start seriously, how very few casualties there were. We had an enormous number of shrouds sent round for us to use, and of course we expected gas.[6]

Regardless of how much preparation or training they had had, air raid wardens, firemen, and other emergency workers had to face very heavy bombing. For instance in Hackney, in the East End, but not as close to the river where the heaviest bombing took place, there were 34 bomb incidents on September 7: 21 of them involved high explosive bombs, 9 unexploded bombs, 3 incendiaries, and 1 delayed action.[7] Bombed-out Londoners were often sent to nearby schools as rest centres. But they were not any safer there than anywhere else. At the Tower Bridge police station, a police sergeant named Peters reported,

> The first major incident to which I attended was at Keeton's Road School. The people had been evacuated from Rotherhithe owing to the docks being well on fire, and some were taken into Keeton's Road School [in Bermondsey] along with their belongings and their families and food. Soon after ten o'clock a bomb fell on the school. ... I, with another officer, was

> searching amongst the debris and after a while my brother officer bent down and pulled something out. He thought it was a piece of bread, but it turned out to be part of a small child, the upper part, the upper limbs of a small child. This so upset us that we came out into the street. There were a number of bodies lying on the footway and in the road. … Eventually some of them stood up, and to my relief they were not all dead. But there were some of them who were dead.[8]

Further down the Thames, near Blackheath, a devout 68-year-old Methodist, Mrs Anne Shepperd, recorded events in a diary. In the last week in August, it is clear how many small raids there were before the big one of September 7. She continually noted the sounding of the sirens, generally about three a day, signalling a raid. After varying lengths of time the All Clear would sound. At home, she sheltered in her own cellar; she also brought the beds down, for greater safety, to the ground floor. The services at her church were continually being interrupted and the decision had to be taken whether to go on or not, or whether to adjourn to under the staircase. But she was well aware of the difference on the night of the 7th.

> It has been a terrible raid this time. Planes look like black clouds so thick they were. Explosions and diving planes seemed endless. … Now great banks of smoke are rolling over and reflections of big fires. … We did not attempt to undress so we were ready when the siren went again an hour later quickly followed by heavy crashes and gun fire which meant cellar at once until early morning. Terrible night. SUNDAY MORNING woke at 10 am but hurried through and got to service about 50 people there. Rev F Hart the preacher, very helpful.[9]

One East End area that was particularly devastated was Poplar, where 132 incidents occurred in the two raids. The bombing was so extensive that following the first All Clear early Saturday evening, there was virtually a mass exodus, either to the West End, which was considered by many to be safer, or into the countryside further east in Essex. Cotter, the Deputy Chief Air Raid Warden of the borough, reported that people were leaving in droves, "Pony carts, hand-drawn barrows, perambulators and cycles with heavily laden carriers, all rolled out of the borough in a steady stream."[10]

There was some panic, and many were determined to leave London altogether. That Saturday Mary Price headed for the hopfields of Kent, where many a Cockney went hop-picking as a sort of paid holiday, and from where some had just returned.

> We didn't know where to go and what to do. The only thing we could think of was to get to Kent to the hop fields, at least we'd be safe getting out of London. Some cousins of mine came round, they'd borrowed a lorry and they said, "Come on, we're going," and I just took two bags of clothes with my five-months-old baby and we made our way to Kent. Now it was just like a convoy of refugees going out. Everything on wheels, old cars, old lorries, anything that moved. It was one steady stream going towards the coast. And we got to Rootham Hill and there was an alarm that some Germans were machine gunning the convoy and we had to get out of the lorry and into the ditch.... Got back on and we finally got to the hop fields and there's this wonderful sense of peace.[11]

Gladys Streilitz and her family in East Ham also decided to get out of London, but the bombing was so heavy that the bus they were on would go no further than Bow. "So the only place to go was to run under this crypt, under this big church. And there the sight that met my eyes, it overcome me. Because there was people praying, and crying and asking God to help us, because there was bombs going on and this crypt, it was actually shuddering. And, well, it was too much for me, I just passed out."[12]

One gleans a sense of how close the East Enders came to disintegration, and that hysteria might have taken over. Violet Regan, whose husband was in the Heavy Rescue Squad in Millwall, wrote an account years later of that first night and morning. Her husband had gone off when the raids started. "I helped to calm my terrified neighbour and her three little children who were screaming with fright and stayed with them until her parents arrived. Then I went to my own shelter. For a very long time I sat listening to the awful bedlam going on outside. … During short lulls I heard the crying of terrified children and the voices of agonised parents trying to soothe them." Her own children had been evacuated to Oxfordshire. Then, because a time bomb had fallen near an oil-storage tank, everyone was instructed to go to the school on Glengall Road.

> I remember so vividly walking to that school carrying one of my neighbour's children wrapped in blankets. Great canopies of billowing smoke blotted out the sun, and barrage balloons were falling down in flames. We were obliged to slap out sparks that alighted on us from all directions. … Everybody settled as comfortably as conditions would allow on the cold concrete floor and the people sat facing each other with our backs propped up against the rough surface of the wall. … It was the awful helplessness that was hardest to bear. We felt like sitting ducks. … Sticks of bombs whistled down and the air was literally torn apart in a loud rushing noise as they

> sped earthward. Everybody instinctively crouched. Holding my breath in an agony of suspense I waited for the blast fully expecting to be blown to pieces. The bombs exploded, rocking the great building to its foundations but by some miracle the school escaped unscathed and nobody was hurt. But the awful expectancy had been too much and I sensed a rising panic as the overwrought women burst into tears and the little ones sensing their fear began to scream.

Singing was the remedy and Vi's father led everyone in "Just a Song at Twilight." When at last the All Clear went they emerged to see the destruction all about. Her house was still standing, but all the windows were blown out. "Conditions were made worse by the severe lack of food, sleep, and clean water. The fires still raged and the smells caused by smouldering ruins were truly unbelievable."[13]

Robert Baltrop, as part of a programme on Thames TV on the Blitz in 1990, provided almost a summary of the effect of September 7 on the East End. He captures well the feeling of the expected at last taking place, and yet the surprise that the big raid had finally started. "There was this sense of it's happened at last. We were taken by surprise, because of all the warnings and no raids, . . . by the size of it." He was working at the grocer's shop Sainsbury's and had been assigned to be a watcher on the roof. He saw the planes arriving "like a swarm of flies." "I had almost a stage view of it sitting up there on the roof, watching them flying across the Thames, coming in." He observed the bombs falling, the fires, the smoke, and not surprisingly the manager decided to close the shop. Baltrop had a date, and felt it was rather romantic to meet during the raid, but his girl informed him that she was instructed to bring him home and join her family in its Anderson shelter. "Being squashed there together and the raid going on and her father talked in gloomy tones about H. G. Wells and how we should all have to live underground."

About 11, there was a lull and he took the three-mile walk to his house, arriving there about 1 a.m. He reported his father's conversation. "How grievingly he talked about the East End and the people in it and what they must be suffering, and then we went to bed, and the raid was still going on, and should we wake up in the morning what would tomorrow be like?" Even that first night, Baltrop appeared to take the raid in his stride, at least as he looked back 50 years later. "After the first Saturday the siren would go about half-past six every evening, and there was a sense of – oh, here it is, the night's begun. And it lasted all night, and the 'all clear' wouldn't go until we were getting ready to go to work in the morning, at seven or half-past seven, something like that. And there was this expectation, so here it is again, we're in for another night of it."[14]

Another observer, S. M. S. Woodcock, was working at an electrical substation near the Woolwich Arsenal.

> The red glow from the flames was a grand but most frightening sight after dark and one felt that the east of London was gone for good. ... None of those at the sub-station expected to survive but when the all-clear went at 6.30 a.m. the damage was seen to be nothing like as serious as they had imagined. ... At 6.45 a.m. an Italian ice-cream merchant appeared & all the children & others from houses round about crow[d]ed round & cleared out his stock in a few minutes. Everyone was rather "white about the gills" but soon recovered their cheerfulness.[15]

Although the East End, its great docks and warehouse areas, and its tenements were the major targets, bombs fell all over London. The better-off parts of the city suffered far less seriously, although the experience could be, for some, deeply traumatic. George Beardmore, an insurance man and would-be novelist who lived in North Harrow with his wife, recorded in his diary for September 10: "Following what must have been the most dangerous and was certainly the most terrifying weekend of our joint lives we have emerged unscathed and with a feeling of triumph because our nerves are still normally responsive."[16]

The *Daily Herald* journalist Mea Allan wrote a running letter on the 7th to her friend May in Oban about her experience. Allan was living in Charlton Mansions off the Strand in central London and remained in it during the first raid and part of the second, not taking shelter until later in the night. She wrote while the raid was going on (by the light of candles, having turned off the electricity) as a way of calming her nerves. (She would eventually be bombed out of her flat in an October raid.)

> There has been a succession of thuds. … They sure are determined – thud – to bomb this fair city. … Fire engines have been tearing about in the streets. thud thud. Wish the guns would go. … Can you hear a zzrr zrr zrr – that's a Jerry prowling about. Where's our GUNS! … I wish I had the guts to go & do some work during all this, but one can do nothing but LISTEN. … A screaming bomb came down that was just too near for comfort. There are fires. … St James's Park, Victoria Street.

She sought shelter in the basement of the flats in the early hours of the morning, reporting to her friend on the hearing of more "thuds."

Allan ended her long letter, "Only hope the same performance won't happen on successive nights until the war ends. It is all right now that it's over, but it was a nightmare come true while the show lasted. Real bombs dropping – there's a war going on & this is it."[17]

Among those who conveyed the feeling of the day was Doris Pierce, then a young woman in Battersea. She had just started work at a department store, the Army & Navy on Victoria Street: "Mum decided to have a shopping trip to Clapham Junction after lunch." They were still there when the alarm sounded, and they headed to a shelter. "After being there about ten minutes someone told us there was a dog-fight up above, so most of us came out to watch. A lot more planes were involved and the clear blue of the sky was strikingly patterned with vapour trails. Mum was getting nervous and said we should go home as quickly as possible." Naturally once there they had tea, and listened to the bombs falling. "Gradually we became aware of a distinct rumbling noise. Dad made the observation that it sounded a bit like the big artillery barrage of the First World War." The family went out to the street. "Here the noise was louder and with it came the smell of burning. Neighbours came out to talk to each other and our faces began to show signs of the fear creeping up on us. ... It was like the most incredible sunset." As it was Saturday night, many would ordinarily have gone to pubs, cinemas or dance halls. Doris might have gone to the dance that night at the Polytechnic on Battersea Park Road, but instead the family went to its Anderson shelter. "We didn't need telling that a bomb had dropped and it was not very far away. ... [It] was obviously designed to create maximum terror, for the screaming noise alone was heart-stopping." It had fallen on a nearby shelter and all were killed, including a passerby. "Someone reported having seen a hand, and other gruesome finds were discovered and a day or so later a body was found on the roof of a house in the next street." She now spent most nights in the family Anderson shelter, although her brother, and the dog and the cat, remained in the house. In fact her brother went out with his mates and "like most lads of his age was enjoying the sense of danger." The cat "was too independent and Rex too excitable. He really loved air raids." The family also sought shelter in the cellar of the nearby flats but were embarrassed by Dad being drunk. In April the family lost everything, but Doris was philosophical about it. "I suppose one can reach the zenith of fear and then the fear starts to lessen."[18]

Ernest Raymond, the popular and highly prolific novelist best known for *Tell England* (1922) about the First World War, was living in Church Row, Hampstead, with a view over London. He was an air raid warden and also in the Home Guard. He wrote that the 7th was "one of the few war dates fixed in our minds forever. And not the date only, but one hour of it: about five o'clock on that September Saturday." But despite the raid, he and his wife went to the theatre to see a revival of John Drinkwater's *Abraham Lincoln*. Also playing that day in the West End were Celia Johnson in Daphne du Maurier's *Rebecca* and Robert Donat in Shaw's *The Devil's Disciple*. There were 24 plays and musicals in the West End at that point, but just one week later only two theatres continued to operate. Raymond remarked, "There was a terrible luminous beauty about that night in London marked by a smell as of burnt oil from the tanks and reservoirs of Dockland." Nevertheless after the play he and his wife went on to the Windsor Dive, near Victoria Station and then back to their flat.[19]

One soldier, stationed in Kent, had an overnight pass that Saturday. He could not find public transport and was offered a lift to the West End by a chauffeured car. "As we moved off a great pall of thick, black smoke billowed across the road, and a fruity voice from the rear seat said 'Do you think it is time I put my tin hat on, John?' 'Yes, Sir,' replied the driver with a touch of Jeeves in his voice. I travelled in great style to the West End. I never knew who my benefactors were, but I found their sang-froid well worth imitating when later in the war moments of crisis and danger arose."[20] Another notable performance that night, not in the West End, was Gounod's *Faust* in Islington at Sadler's Wells. While *Faust* was being performed, the theatre's director, Tyrone Guthrie, and others were on the roof watching the raid. When the opera finished, the audience emerged from the artistic presentation of Hell to see its visual representation in the burning of the docks. The theatre closed for the rest of the war, becoming a residence until 1941 (when it suffered minor bomb damage) for about 180 locals who had lost their homes. It did not reopen as a theatre until June 7, 1945, with the world premiere of Benjamin Britten's greatest opera, *Peter Grimes*.[21]

Westminster, at the very centre of London, was affected by the bombings, but not until the late evening. At first it all seemed a bit removed from the action. William Sansom wrote quite lyrically about the day. He became a very well-known writer and played Barrett, the "new boy," in Humphrey Jennings's masterpiece depicting the Fire Service during the Blitz, *Fires Were Started*. He himself was actually a fireman, as were all those who played them in the film. Sansom also wrote one of the best-known stories of the war, "The Wall," about the collapse of a wall during a fire, killing a fireman. He gave a vivid account of September 7 in his *The Blitz: Westminster at War*: "So then, the dawning of that fatal seventh. One of the fairest days of the century, a day of clear warm air and high blue skies. Over the capital on the eve of its threatened siege there dawdled a forgotten sense of peace." Indeed, the feel of the day seems to have intrigued many. One RAF officer remarked,

"It was a bit like one of those Westerns where one of the cowboys comments 'It's too quiet. I don't like it.' And then an arrow goes thunk into his back."[22]

Sansom's account continues:

> The hours on such a day in high summer seem to extend themselves in their invitation to leisure, the trees in full leaf cast in their dusty shadows a truth of peace greater than transient human wars; and … in many men's troubled, taut minds there was yet an appreciation of that queer lullaby of peace brought with the weather, an evocation of London summers of the past, when striped awnings shaded the shopping and geraniums bloomed red in window boxes freshly painted and blistered in the sun, when bands played in the royal parks and canaries slept in the tenement windows, when this central part of London was a fine and spacious vista of pale grey, black, green and scarlet.
>
> Towards six o'clock the fiction of unease became fact, the man on the street learnt that something had been happening in the East End, something more significant than the ordinary tidings brought by the siren. … The docks were ablaze. And as the sun set, those in the West End streets grew conscious of the unbelievable, for the sunset occurred not only in the accustomed West near Putney and Willesden, but also incredibly in the East over St. Paul's and where the City of London was held to lie. That was curious enough – but when the western skies had grown already dark the fierce red glow in the East stuck harshly fast and there was seen for the first time that black London roofscape silhouetted against what was to become a monotonously copper-orange sky. So in Westminster they knew and they could see that something

was on. Yet still it seemed curiously separate. This was yet happening in the East.

Just after eleven o'clock, the first large cluster of bombs fell in the West End, about five bombs near Victoria Station, causing casualties and death. Sansom said,

> The powdered smell of smashed plaster and brick poisoned the air for the first time. Glass, illimitable, spread itself across the pavements and out over the road – it seemed to lie two or three inches thick. The peace was shattered, and the machine of defence went into action for its first real blooding. It was an unlucky time – the public houses had just closed. Many people were just out then on the pavements, for at the end of the Vauxhall Bridge Road there was a busying of late night trams and buses. The iron replica of Big Ben stood then above a scene of stunned disaster and wounding, cries were heard from the neighbouring street, and in the great darkened railway station itself there occurred particular trouble. … This first sight of blood and wounding is an experience sharp in its emotional effect, often physically affecting.[23]

Nevertheless, those areas outside the East End were in that first 12 hours more observers than participants. Meanwhile, one can sense a difference between the responses of British citizens and Americans living in London in an emotional account by an American resident, Mrs E. H. Cotton, living in a flat near Regent's Park. I don't know when she wrote this diary-like account but it must have been some time later. She was a young mother at the time of the war, and she had composed her reminiscence for her granddaughter and in memory of her son-in-law. Dating her entry

September 8, she wrote about the previous night's raid, "When and where bombs fall and create havoc and death, this is called an 'Incident.' Good old British understatement. ... So many casualties have resulted from all this Hell." She and her husband had gone to Letchworth for a visit.

> We were all placidly at tea in the garden there when the wireless announced that London was having another air-raid. Well, raid or no raid, we must return to London – and the sooner we got under cover there the better. ... Driving into London was like driving into a fortress. And it sounded like one as evening fell. After dinner we went upstairs to a friend's flat on the 6th floor in order to see the Big Fire, for the Nazis have really hit a few things in Dockland at last. ... In the clear night air Central London lay silhoueted [sic] before us against a slate blue sky. And, to the left, a pulsing curtain of orange and scarlet, shot with flame, hung like the monstrous backdrop of a nightmare presentation. "HELL ON EARTH" by Hitler and Goering Act I "London's burning – London's burning," buzzed senselessly in my head, and I kept thinking of how my mother had been in the Great Chicago Fire when a little girl – and of how she used to tell us about it when we were children, my brothers and me. The fire still burns today. And at noon a broadcast gave nearly 460 dead and over 1,000 injured. That is Calamity – and Tragedy – and Death![24]

In Kensington, Joan Wyndham was planning, under the stimulus of the raid, the termination of her virginity. Midnight on September 7 found her in an air-raid shelter with the literary figure Sir John Squire

> roaring tight, sitting opposite me next to his Scotch Presbyterian cook. … Squire keeps saying he wants to read Wodehouse's *Uncle Fred in Springtime* once more before he dies. The bombs are lovely, I think it is all thrilling. Nevertheless, as the opposite of death is life, I think I shall get seduced by Rupert tomorrow. Rowena has promised to go to a chemist's with me and ask for Volpas Gels, just in case the French thingummy isn't foolproof. … The all-clear went at five a.m. All clear for my lovely Rupert, I thought. … As it was Sunday, we all went to church – funny how devout people look after an air-raid.

The next afternoon she went to Rupert's flat and got on with it. "Rupert slipped off his clothes, and I suddenly realised he looked terribly funny in the nude and began laughing helplessly. 'What's the matter, don't you like my cock?' he asked, rather taken aback. 'It's all right,' I said, 'just a bit lop-sided!' 'Most people's are – never mind, take your clothes off.'" Afterwards she "thought 'Well, that's done, and I'm glad it's over! If that's really all there is to it I'd rather have a good smoke or go to the pictures.' … In spite of it all being rather disappointing, I still love Rupert more than I can bear and would do anything for him."[25]

Miss N. Bosanquet had a more conventional Blitz experience in Kensington. She wrote a long diary letter from 38 Kensington Park Road to "My dear Mummie." During the afternoon alert she continued with her errands, including having identification photographs made. By the time she arrived home the warning was still on, so she "went to the garden where Mary and Mrs G were standing by the shelter ready to pop in." They heard a bomb falling so they entered the Anderson shelter, but went back to the house after five and made tea.

> The kettle was just boiling when another warning went so we took tea out with us & had it in peace. … The shelter is crammed with rugs & cushions, – Mary & Mrs G on two chairs & me opposite them on a rug on the steps. Any sort of bed or bunk would be utterly impossible, & so would sleep. … I also rang up my ambulance station (– here comes a plane) and offered myself at night time for the next ten days. … The more I see of Londoners the more I admire their amazing calmness. True they all look a trifle white & tired, but not drawn and most cheerful & ordinary.

She next notes,

> 10.35. My God! This is hellish! Over went a plane just now & dropped about six bombs, each one swishing as it dropped. I just crouch terror stricken with an eiderdown up around my ears. … 11.50 Well – we're still alive anyway & honestly I don't find it so alarming except when bombs fall. … It is marvellous how safe one feels in here – a nice safe little nutshell, half buried in the ground … 1.50 Fancy that. I think I now consider myself quite case-hardened. A bomb came whooshing down then & exploded about as far away as the bottom of Church Street, and I didn't bother to cover my ears for it. … 5.50 The all-clear has gone & I am going to bed. … It was a long, long night, and beastly uncomfortable. … I feel myself having survived last night I can survive anything. Also I shant find to-night half as alarming as I shall know just what to expect. Mary had thoroughly unnerved me for it by telling me of the swish, swish of bombs all round you – which certainly happens & is horrible, but nothing is so bad once you have heard its voice.[26]

Having weathered the first raid in North London, Barbara Nixon, the actress working as a warden, thought that was that, and went off to dinner in Soho. "When we came out of the restaurant we stopped aghast. The whole sky to the east was blazing red. The afternoon spectacle was completely dwarfed; it seemed as though half of London must be burning. … I realised that the whole of London was a target area, and that Piccadilly and King's Cross were as important as the Albert Dock, and any street might get its share."

People returned to the shelters for the second raid but "very few of them imagined that they would have to sit in a shelter for more than an hour or so; neither for that matter, and more inexcusably, had the authorities. … The overcrowding was appalling, and the air stank. …"[27]

In Chelsea, the sirens sounded again at 8:35 p.m. Jo Oakman had been at the cinema. She heard about the Cadogan House Shelter being directly hit during the raid, and on September 10 she recorded the consequences in her diary as she greeted another dawn: "Official number for the Cadogan House Shelter is 57. Some crushed beyond recognition and in pulp. Heaven help us all! … God! What a day dawning! Peace after a night of hell but what a price. Over 41 poor dead things." That weekend Londoners moved from a casual giddiness to almost a sense of relief that the heavy raids had at last started and could be survived, but then fairly rapidly dread and horror might take over. Next, as the raids went on, one became used to them and relaxed somewhat, while realizing how serious the attacks were. Years later, a friend of Jo Oakman wrote about his work with her as a warden. "[Our] lives at that time [were] punctuated by bangs, so that in the end one became casual about them, regrettable though that may be, because in most instances they meant death or injury to someone."[28]

In his quiet way, the writer E. M. Forster supported the war effort. His characteristically muted response had already been put forth in his well-known 1938 essay, "What I Believe" in which he had given two cheers for Democracy as, with all its defects, the best system available. In his view, only Love, the Beloved Republic, deserved three. He lived primarily in Abinger in the Surrey countryside, but he did have a small flat on Turnham Green in Chiswick, to be near where his policeman lover, Bob Buckingham, lived. Forster had become a good friend of the younger writer Christopher Isherwood. Isherwood and W. H. Auden had caused great offence by leaving England for the United States before war broke out and declining to return. Forster wrote to Isherwood on September 11 describing the raid. "I saw the first night of it [the Blitz] last Saturday from my flat. ... London burning, a grandiose spectacle. ... I am certainly very sad and apprehensive. I am sure that we are going to be invaded. ... The night as I write is full of booming bombers. I wish I was out of it all – not in another part of the world, which would not suit me, but dead. I am sure there is hope, but want someone else to do the hoping."[29]

That same day Forster noted in his diary:

> I watched this event ... with disgust and indignation, but with no intensity though the spectacle was superb. I thought "It is nothing like the burning of Troy." Yet the Surrey Docks were ablaze at the back with towers and spires outlined against them, greenish yellow searchlights swept the sky in futile agony, crimson shells burst behind the spire of Turnham Green church. This is all that a world catastrophe amounts to. Something which one is too sad and sullen to appreciate.[30]

After the second raid started, the Rev. Mohan heard that another bomb had fallen in Linden Grove, near his vicarage in Penge, and he went to find out how some parishioners were at 10 Linden Grove.

> I found a barricade across the road but the policeman let me go down to find which house had been hit. I found No. 9 flattened out completely & the Simkins' house was destroyed beyond repair. The roof had collapsed & the upper floor ruined. ... Returned home to await a quiet time before going to Beckenham Hospital to make enquiries about the Simkins. Went out later & found that Mervyn was in the Hospital with a bruised shoulder & shock & would be going home tomorrow. Mrs. Simkin had gone home – though as her home is destroyed I suppose that means to a friend's house. The other two boys, Desmond & Peter, were apparently not at home at the time of the raid.

At 11:10 he went to bed, apparently with no consideration that he might go to a shelter, and presumably not having an Anderson shelter in his garden. He commented on hearing bombs nearby. "Got up at 2.45 & made tea. Raiders have been over us continuously & dropping many bombs too near for my liking! ... I got up at 6 a.m. and cooked my breakfast. Peter Simkin rang up & I went & met Mrs S. & Desmond & Peter & brought them back to the Vicarage." And then, rather touchingly, the three Simkins signed their names in Rev. Mohan's diary: Ethel A. Simkin, Desmond P. M. Simkin, Roland P. Simkin, presumably known as Peter.[31]

One of the most vivid accounts of the Blitz was written by 18-year-old Colin Perry in his wartime diary. He recorded the weekend of September 7 and 8 as one entry. "This is the most momentous weekend. Yesterday I lived through my most momentous day – so far." His aim was to travel by bicycle in the London suburbs and observe what was going on with his binoculars. The siren had sounded. At first he only saw British fighters but then there were bombs.

> Pandemonium broke loose right above me. ... It was the most amazing, riveting sight. Directly above me were literally hundreds of 'planes, Germans! ... My ears were deafened by bombs, machine-gun fire, the colossal inferno of machine after machine zooming in the blue sky. ... I would not disown these minutes for Life itself. Zooommmmm, eeeoooohh-hhhooooowwww, rururururururrrr – engine after engine, machine-gun after machine-gun, boump after boump. ... The densest, biggest cloud of smoke I have ever seen formed itself on the skyline of London.

He went home, continued to observe, slept in his bed, and didn't take shelter. "Despite the worst air-raid in history I secured a good night's sleep." The special news broadcast on Sunday morning did not hide the deaths and the destruction. Perry reported the news: "Thousands of refugees from the smitten quarters were bombed as they fled. Mothers lay protectingly over their children in the gutters under the glow of the fires as the Nazi bombers rained down death. Fire-fighters worked through hell. All those sights of pitiful Spain, China, Finland are left behind compared with this tragedy of London."[32]

Some of those who recorded the events of that day conveyed the depth of the personal impact, not only a loss or a questioning of religious faith, but also the trauma that might endure for decades. Viola Bawtree's tone is now far less contained: "The All Clear did not sound till 5 a.m. ... What an inferno of a night! I felt all raw and bleeding." And Monday afternoon: "I'm in danger of losing God. … Oh, I can't write for tears – I feel as though nothing matters any more & prayer seems utterly futile. I don't think I'll ever lose my belief in God but I'm cut right off from Him now in a nightmare world."[33]

On Sunday Len Jones left the shelter early to go home.

> I went out to see how our house was, and when I got there the front door was lying back, and the glass of the windows had fallen in, and I could see the top of the house had virtually disappeared. Inside, everything was blown to pieces, you could see it all by the red glow reflecting from the fires that were raging outside. Then I looked out the back and suddenly I realized that where my father's shed and workshop used to be, was just a pile of rubble, bricks. Then I saw two bodies, two heads sticking up. I recognized one head in particular; it was a Chinese man, Mr Say, he had one eye closed, and then I began to realize that he was dead. … When I saw the dead Chinese, I just convulsed and couldn't get my breath. I was shaking completely. Then I thought well I must be dead, as they were, so I struck a match, and tried to burn my finger, I kept doing this with a match to see if I was still alive. I could see, but I thought I cannot be alive, this is the end of the world. The fires were everywhere and everything you looked at was red, sheer heat, blood, the lot. That night haunted me for more than forty years, it was so awful I couldn't tell anybody about it, it almost destroyed me.[34]

V

Civil Defence

"You just headed for the glow in the sky"

STARTING on September 7 and continuing throughout the Blitz, all parts of the vast network of the Civil Defence Services were on the domestic "front line," coping with the results of the German air raids. This included especially the air raid wardens and firemen, for whom that Saturday was the beginning of a veritable and extreme trial by fire. But it also included the police as well as other units such as Heavy Rescue and Light Rescue, Ambulance and Home Guard.[1]

The Rescue Services had the particularly onerous and dangerous task of removing buried and probably wounded individuals from bombed buildings. Once the Blitz started, it was clear that this branch of the Civil Defence was understaffed. The number of civilians who needed help to get out of their houses after each night's raid had been underestimated. In addition, the planners had also overstaffed the services designed to deal with the dead – as it turned out, there were far fewer mortalities than expected.

These were of course just two of many miscalculations government planners had made. We have already seen how, even as the groundwork was laid in the late 1930s, the authorities misjudged the types of air raids Great Britain would suffer; in addition, the shelters, a key component of the civil defence system, were inadequate. For those without Anderson shelters in their backyards, the provision of communal public shelters was based on erroneous premises – that air raids would be short, would take place in daylight, and that the shelters would need to be occupied comparatively briefly. The very first public shelters, trench shelters in London's parks, were unreassuring and always damp. Once the Blitz started, those who went to public shelters – and many remained at home, either in the Anderson shelters, or under the stairs, or in their beds – came early and remained for the night. Some shelterers brought along personal treasures, increasing the crowding. Little provision for sanitation had been made in the early days and the number of people jammed together in the shelters meant that they were extremely crowded and extremely smelly.

Brick and concrete street shelters constructed above ground in the East End were designed to hold about 50 people. It turned out that they were poorly built, and the potential users quite rightly did not trust them. When tested by raids, these shelters frequently collapsed even if they were not directly hit. As has been mentioned, those in the East End seeking shelter were far more likely to trek to Epping Forest, to tube stations (frequently overcrowded) or department store basements in the West End. Quite a few went to the caves at Chislehurst in Kent, where they established "rooms" with furniture. Far less appealing was the terrible Tilbury shelter, a massive underground storage area down the Thames where eventually around 15,000 people congregated nightly. The filth and the stench were overwhelming. The "people" were coming together, but ironically (though not surprisingly under such conditions), hatred flared, most notably toward Jews, who were seen as "pushy" and fighting for the best spots, or for being the first to flee as the most prone to panic, "another yid saving his skin."[2]

Yet Vincent Sheean, the American journalist, wrote about his visits to the tube shelters in *Between the Thunder and the Sun* (1943):

> The poorest and dirtiest of the East End Cockneys are not (by the conditions of their life) permitted to develop the most admirable characteristics. They are not heroes; neither are they bulldogs. They sniveled and quaked under the bombs, huddled together in their filth like so many frightened animals. Could it be otherwise? I only went to these deep shelters once or twice to see what they were like, and came out again almost choked by the smells.[3]

The Ministry of Health feared that because of raids many would become psychotic. It made the easy but unwarranted assumption that Jews and foreigners would be the most likely to panic.[4] The *Jewish Chronicle* wrote that the Jews of the East End had shown "sustained and unwavering courage," and noted – quite erroneously – that "Hitler has bombed anti-Semitism out of many districts in East London where once it was rife." The paper's editorial on September 13 began:

> Of all the major blunders perpetrated by Hitler in the war, and they are many, history will probably condemn the present savage attack on London as the greatest, as it assuredly is the most wanton and criminal. Heralded by a speech full of sound and fury and suggesting in almost every sentence a haunting fear of defeat, it suggests by its sheer insensate and undiscriminating fury the rage of a baffled and beaten tyrant.[5]

It would take quite a few years for these words to be fully justified.

The government did not come close to predicting how many homes would be destroyed by German bombing, let alone addressing where all the newly homeless citizens should go. On top of the immense problems about where people were to go and stay, there was the additional complication of bombs which fell on London and didn't detonate, although they were still "live." There were 3,000 of these UXBs dealt with during the Blitz. This meant that streets had to be cordoned off and evacuated while the bombs were being defused, even though the houses on the street were untouched. As a result, many more civilians were temporarily homeless (or permanently so, if the UXB squad didn't succeed).

Virtually no provision had been made for those who didn't have a place to stay. The number of homeless in London – ultimately at least 1.5 million – was equivalent to how many people the authorities had expected would be *killed* by the air raids. Corpses would have been far easier to deal with than the dispossessed, and had received far more careful thought from the authorities. London was not at all ready for the systematic bombing that started on September 7.

After that first weekend, as one report by Mass Observation pointed out: "Of course, the press versions of life going on normally in the East End on Monday are grotesque. There was no bread, no electricity, no milk, no gas, no telephones. ... There was no understanding in the huge buildings of Central London for the tiny crumbled streets of densely massed population. Here people wanted to be brave but found bravery was something purely negative, cheerless, and without encouragement or prospect of success."[6] The emergency services found it extremely difficult to cope with such a heavy and endless raid. The first aid stations were badly equipped and couldn't deal with the walking wounded and it was very difficult for vehicles – fire engines, ambulances – to get through the bombed streets.

Once the heavy raids began on London the air raid wardens were invaluable, contrary to what had appeared to be the case before. Lady Violet Bonham Carter, the lively daughter of Herbert Asquith, the Liberal Prime Minister during the first half of the First World War, wrote in November 1940 in the *Spectator*,

> During the year of lull before the *Blitzkrieg* started Air-Raid Wardens were generally regarded as a quite unnecessary and rather expensive nuisance. It was difficult to see what they were there for. They appeared to spend their days in basements, listening to gas-lectures in the intervals of playing darts, and when they emerged at nightfall it was only to worry innocent people about their lights. They occasionally held up the traffic by performing strange charades, pretending as best they could to cope with imaginary situations of wild improbability. And for this life of idleness and antics the public heard with horror that some of them were actually paid.
>
> As an [unpaid] participator in that year of waiting broken by antics, I felt some sympathy with the public. Our training was tedious; it often seemed academic, sometimes even absurd. I could never manage to persuade myself, that confronted with a bombed and blazing house from which gas and water were escaping and in which "persons" were "trapped" I should meticulously fill in an elaborate printed form with block letters describing under the appropriate headings not only what had, but also what had not, happened. Like many others I often longed for a less hypothetical, more immediate task.
>
> Today we have our reward. We are conscious, as never before in our lives, of fulfilling a definite, direct and essential function. We are a front-line service, in action every night in the defence of London. We know that our neighbours in

> every walk of life turn to us in their hour of need and look on us as their friends. We would not exchange our jobs for any other.[7]

Most wardens were well regarded, but, of course, there were exceptions. One person remembered one such on the 7th, as the German bombers began their attack: "Then Gus said to me, 'Cor, look at those bombs falling,' and the Gasometers at Bromley by Bow went up in flames. ... It seemed as though we were watching a movie. ... In the meantime our brave ARP warden, who for months had been swaggering about in his uniform, tin helmet cocked to one side, was cringing against the wall under the concrete steps, sobbing. I never saw that man again."[8]

Nevertheless, in the vast majority of cases, the air raid wardens played an important role in coping with the Blitz. They were ordinary people who, faced with an emergency situation, rose to the occasion and performed, on the whole, calmly and indeed heroically. In the East End, with its suspicion of authority, they might have some difficulty. The wardens themselves reflected their community, and the wardens in Poplar could be a rather tough lot.

> We had a very rough-and-ready crowd indeed. If they liked you they probably called you "mate" irrespective of your rank; if they thought you were just passable they'd call you "mister," and if they disliked you they usually called you "sir." There was only one thing kept 'em together – they had a kind of discipline imposed by themselves, and that was the fear that their mates wouldn't think that a man was doing the job.[9]

In this area, as in many others, a major factor in preserving morale

5. A public shelter on Clapham Common.

was, no matter how frightened one might actually be, to maintain a front as best one could, to not show fear and to take the situation as calmly as possible, indeed to underplay and understate it. And the wardens themselves were not to take shelter, other than going into them to check how things were going. This, of course, put them at considerable risk. In the shelter itself there was supposed to be – but frequently wasn't – a shelter marshal in charge.

Barbara Nixon published her account of being an air raid warden. Questions can be asked about her narrative, as they can of all the other accounts one encounters. Does it fit into the myth of the Blitz? Did the myth suppress the less heroic parts of the story? Did it only come into full bloom once the war was over? Nixon was a part-time volunteer and shared responsibility for 17 shelters. As she notes, the conditions in the shelters were "appalling. In many boroughs there were only flimsy surface shelters, with no light, no seats, no lavatories, and insufficient numbers even of these."[10]

She was also responsible for reporting bombs that fell in her area and with enforcing the blackout. To a degree, the wardens were firemen as well, as they would work on putting out small fires. (And if that wasn't enough, one warden remarked: "We all had an order to watch out for parachutists coming down in the area."[11]) According to Nixon, there was even less training than Lady Violet had received. She remembered that the instruction provided little information about how to deal with gas, shelters or incendiary bombs. "There was no lecture on what a warden was supposed to do, either in raids or lulls; there was no lecture on what other C[ivil] D[efence] services were supposed to do, or how the Control Room worked, how an incident should be controlled, what rules existed in regard to public shelters, or the relationship of the warden and the shelter marshal; there was no instruction about the various report forms, and not even rudimentary first aid. . . . Armed with a tin hat and a whistle, I, and hundreds of others, faced the blitzes which burst on us on September 7th, 1940. Our only asset was our zeal to help."[12]

Although it did not happen until the second week of the Blitz, perhaps the most powerful moment in Nixon's narrative is an account of her first "incident," the first time she did more than observe distant bombings and fire. It occurred slightly outside her district, and though she didn't know the buildings or their occupants, it was where she happened to find herself one afternoon and as a warden she felt she should try to help. It was there she encountered her first death, a particularly tragic one. She didn't know if her emotions would be under control. "I was not let down lightly. In the middle of the street lay the remains of a baby. It had been blown clean through the window, and had burst on striking the roadway. To my intense relief, pitiful and horrible as it was, I was not nauseated, and found a torn piece of curtain in which to wrap it."[13]

Also essential to the front line of the home front, beyond the millions of Londoners themselves, were the firemen. They knew firsthand how perilously close Hitler came to achieving his objectives – much closer than the Nazis realized. The fires at the docks were horrendous, intensified by the unfortunate fact that so much timber was stored at the Surrey Commercial Docks; similar combustibles at other docks also burned most merrily, including rum at the West India Dock. There were streams of fire in the Thames as the contents of the docks fell into the river, as well as flaming barges floating out of control. The light of the fires was extraordinary, and provided a dramatic sight from all over London, not to mention that it helped the German planes when they returned for the second raid. One observer noted, "Standing on our porch, facing central London, that evening, we could see to read a newspaper by the light of dockland fires some fifteen miles away."[14]

The fire in the Quebec Yard of the Surrey Docks holds the record for the most intense single fire ever in Britain.

> There were pepper fires, loading the surrounding air heavily with stinging particles, so that when the firemen took a deep breath it felt like burning fire itself. There were rum fires, with torrents of blazing liquid pouring from the warehouse doors and barrels exploding like bombs themselves. There was a paint fire, another cascade of white-hot flame. ... A rubber fire gave forth black clouds of smoke so asphyxiating that it could only be fought from a distance.[15]

The historian of the London Fire Brigade later wrote about these fires, providing some statistical background:

> Four-fifths of the firemen involved had had no prior experience of actual fire-fighting. In normal times a 30-pump fire is a very big fire. Shortly after midnight [that is, the early hours of September 8] there were nine fires in London rating over 100 pumps. In the Surrey docks there were two, of 300 and 130 pumps; at Woolwich Arsenal 200 pumps; at Bishopsgate Goods Yard and at five points on the docks, 100-pump fires. All these were technically "out of control," that is to say unsurrounded, uncontrolled and spreading.[16]

In a book published in 1942, Hannen Swaffer, a very well-known journalist, recorded the experience of one of the "amateur" firemen recruited into service when the war broke out but not incorporated into the regular fire service until 1942. Swaffer was writing very close to the events and his description conformed to the stereotype of the understated heroic reaction. But stereotypes are not necessarily untrue. "Heroism has no boast to make. It is placid and unemotional. It did a job, which it is still doing. And with that it leaves the matter." The account of the two days nonstop from September 7 did not ignore how much went wrong.

> They [the auxiliary firemen] worked on in wet uniforms, that there was no food, that, soaked through, they had nothing to drink but water from the taps, that everything went wrong, that nothing was right, and that they were all dead with fatigue. Few people realize the calamitous inefficiency of the arrangements made for a bombing of London that we had been warned, years before, was inevitable. There were no

> canteens. ... Their hours ... were 112 per week, and the pay was seventy shillings, more than a pound less than that paid to regular firemen whose work they shared, and who were their mates in life and death.[17]

Although they were later amalgamated, at the time the Blitz began, somewhat parallel to the paid and unpaid wardens, the firemen were divided into two sections, the smaller group of professionals, and then, not quite voluntary, but paid at a much lower rate, the auxiliary firemen. At the beginning of the war there were 2,000 professionals in the London Fire Brigade and 23,000 full- and part-time auxiliaries. The part-timers had regular jobs as well, working as firemen one night on duty, one night on call, one night off, as well as doing their daytime jobs. They had had very little experience of fires. The regular firemen treated the auxiliaries rather badly, as second-class citizens. Before September 7 many of them derided the volunteer auxiliary firefighters, with comparatively little to do, as "war dodgers, loafers and parasites."[18]

The firemen did not have extensive opportunities to learn how to fight fires before the bombing became severe, as there were few serious fires before September 7. The biggest previous fire began on August 19, when the Admiralty oil installation on Pembroke Dock was bombed; the resulting fire raged for 17 days. The services did not contain enough men, particularly as they were in intense competition with conscription to the military. The shortage was particularly acute at the officer level.

Firefighting, dangerous in peacetime, was all the more difficult under Blitz conditions. Rather than one fire to be coped with, there were many, and the fires, set by incendiary bombs, themselves provided beacons for the bombers to see by. Not only would firemen be soaking wet within five minutes, they were in almost constant danger of having new bombs fall on or around them. Fires might not be spotted until some time after they started if they were in unoccupied and locked places of business or homes, adding to the difficulty of fighting them. In the case of residences, their occupants might have gone to shelters or indeed left London. The telephone system might be overloaded or destroyed. Messenger boys used at those times had to careen between flaming walls and would frequently be knocked off their bikes. Radio communication did not exist yet. One of these boys, a fire dispatch rider named Stan Hook, remembered that a few hours after the bombing began on Black Saturday, "roads were blocked by bomb craters and fallen buildings and water mains were fractured and electricity was cut off."[19] Brigades from other districts might be called in to help, but they were often unfamiliar with the area. Firefighters eventually were called upon from as far away as Brighton, Rugby and Swindon. Worst of all, water supplies were very uncertain. But as with the wardens, once the firemen were in action, doubts about their ability faded.

The fires of September 7 were the largest London had ever experienced, even bigger than the Great Fire of September 1666. More than a thousand fires raged that night, as they would again on two other nights in September and again once in October. There would be 13,000 fires in London during those two months. Firefighter F. W. Hurd recorded his impressions of September 7, writing in December 1940. He was stationed in Euston and after the first All Clear, his squad was sent to East Ham, a considerable distance, to cope with a serious fire. "As soon as we entered the East End we saw evidence of the raid (the first most of us had seen). Houses were demolished, roads torn up, and a surface shelter had been wrecked."[20] The fires they found there were under control already and the unit was sent on to the East Ham station.

When the second raid started, the unit went to the docks.

> Arriving at the gas-works chaos met our eyes. Gasometers were punctured & were blazing away, a power house had been struck rendering useless the hydraulic hydrant supply (the only source of water there). . . . Then, overhead, we heard "Jerry." . . . I had my first experience of a bomb-explosion. A weird whistling sound & I ducked beside the pump. . . . Then a vivid flash of flame, a column of earth & debris flying into the air, & the ground heaved.

After that, his group was sent a half mile away, to get water from hydrants to fight the fire. Once having done that he had time to take in the scene, proclaiming, "What a sight. About a mile away to our right was the river front. The whole horizon on that side was a sheet of flame." At 3:30 in the morning, a canteen van pulled up and the firefighters had their first food and drink (sandwiches and the omnipresent tea) since midday. But the snack was not to be enjoyed, as Hurd explained:

> Just then the bombing became more severe & localised. A brighter glow was in the sky immediately over us, then we saw the flames. . . . A huge mushroom of flame shot into the air from the docks followed by a dull rolling roar. An oil container had exploded. The whole atmosphere became terrible again with the noise of gunfire. (Afterwards when London established its famous barrage [of anti-aircraft guns] we got used to it, but on that first night it was just Hell.)[21]

They were on duty until 10 a.m. on Sunday, when they were relieved by a crew from Brighton, miles away on the Sussex coast.

Cyril Demarne, who was an officer of the Fire Service, has also given a vivid account of September 7. He was a native of the East End, born in Poplar, and had been with the West Ham Fire Brigade since 1925. Because of a light raid the previous night, he had been up until 4 a.m. On September 7, he reported that the first bombs fell on the Ford Motor Works in Dagenham and then on the Beckton Gas Works, the largest in Europe. He continued:

> Columns of fire pumps, five hundred of them ordered to West Ham alone, sped eastwards to attend fires in ships and warehouses, sugar refineries, soap works, tar distilleries, chemical works, timber stacks, paint and varnish works, the humble little homes of the workers and hundreds of other fires that, in peace time, would have made headline news. Two hundred and fifty acres of tall timber stacks blazed out of control in the Surrey Commercial Docks; the rum quay buildings of the West India Docks, alight from end to end, gushed blazing spirit from their doors. An army of rats ran from a Silvertown soap works; a short distance along the North Woolwich Road, molten pitch from a stricken tar distillery flooded the road, bringing to a halt all emergency vehicles. On the riverside, blazing barges threatened wharves. Some were set adrift by well-intentioned people, only to be swept by the tide downstream, broadside on, to the peril of fire boats, manoeuvring to pump water ashore to feed the land pumps. … Many [firemen] feared their last hour had come but they carried on, encouraged by the example of comrades slogging away at burning buildings, their heads down to protect faces from the scorching heat and flying sparks. … All around them lay a maze of twisting, snaking fire hose. … Many families were buried in the rubble of their homes and

> had to be dug out by rescue squads. . . . Some were beyond aid and scenes of heartrending grief were witnessed as survivors uncovered the mutilated bodies of loved ones. First aid parties moved in, treating the injured and covering the dead with a blanket or whatever came to hand, leaving the body stretched out on the rubble to await collection by a mortuary van. . . . Great blazing embers, carried aloft in the terrific heat upcast, spread fire over the heads of firemen. Powerful jets of water seemed to be turned to steam by the great roaring flames from the timber stacks; all the effort seemed to be in vain; the task was overwhelming.[22]

Ultimately, a thousand pumps were used in the attempt to control the fire at the Surrey Docks.

When Jack Rothmans, a member of the Auxiliary Fire Service stationed near the Surrey Docks, first saw the planes, he thought they were British. "Then we saw the bombs leave the planes, and everyone ran for cover, buildings tossed about, the ground shook, and the next thing we knew the bells were down and away we went." He added later: "The night seemed endless, wave after wave, or what seemed like wave after wave of planes, the roar and cackle of the flames, falling buildings, men shouting."[23] An anonymous fireman at the East India Dock commented: "It was all new, but we were all unwilling to show fear, however much we might feel it. You looked round and saw the rest doing their job. You couldn't let them down, you just had to get on with it." He remembers passing a member of the women's branch of the Auxiliary Fire Service and experiencing the need to act bravely in her eyes, "not taking a blind bit of notice of the stuff that was falling pretty thick all round. Seeing her I strolled past as if I was used to walking out in the middle of bombs every Saturday afternoon."[24]

The mixture of professionalism and amateurism, the spirit of all hands to the pumps, was captured by A. P. Herbert, the well-known humour writer, who was also a Member of Parliament. He was helping the war effort by running his *Water Gypsy* as a patrol craft on the Thames. It was a 38-foot motor launch, docked in a little pier at the bottom of his garden at Hammersmith. He was part of the civilian River Emergency Service, an amateur organization of private boat owners. On September 7, he was busy celebrating his wife's birthday. Once the raid started, he and a member of his crew who was at the party travelled down the Thames, heading toward the havoc at the docks. "I kept thinking, 'I ought to be frightened. I don't seem to be. Why is this?' The answer was, I suppose, that, whatever happened, I knew I should not be buried by a mass of masonry or perish slowly pinned by an iron girder."

He was commissioned to pull a tug. Generally at night it was too dark on the river but because of the fires "the Pool was like Piccadilly in the good old days."[25] The tug, hence easily found, turned out to be empty so Herbert didn't tow it. He was next commissioned to deliver wire to Woolwich to be used to capture and tow the out-of-control floating flaming barges. He was cautioned that he wouldn't be able to get through because of the fires and because so many ships had been sunk in the river, but he ignored these bits of information. "The wind was westerly, and the accumulated smoke and sparks of all the fires swept in a high wall right across the river. There was not a soul to be seen. ... The scene was like a lake in Hell. Burning barges were drifting everywhere. ... It was something to be the only boat in Hell." He delivered the wire and on his return to Westminster, "we found Hell in a more reasonable condition."[26]

The firemen were understated heroes of the moment. Jim Goldsmith, a regular fireman from a station in the City, reported on his experiences:

> You didn't need any lights or maps to find the way, you just headed for the glow in the sky. It was real chaos, buildings ablaze all round and the worst of all seeing houses flattened by the bombs. If anyone said they could not feel fear that night they must be lying through their teeth. ... There were sad and funny moments mixed though. We found a woman crying her eyes out as her house had been damaged by the bombing, it seemed her doors and windows had blown out. As we were trying to pacify her, another elderly lady came along and said "What's up, love?" The first lady was telling her all about the damage when the second one said "Never mind love, let's go in and try and make a cup of tea." ... If anyone tells you how wonderful war is, let them have a go at putting bodies together, and try and explain to someone who has lost a relative. The smell of burning wood and the stench of burning flesh is a thing you will never forget.[27]

Not surprisingly, there was a degree of hyperbole at the time, although in keeping with the English style, it was not too much overblown. One pardonable exception, perhaps, was Hannen Swaffer, writing in the anthology *Went the Day Well*. He suggested that in this war there should be an Unknown Civilian, one of the 25,000 auxiliary firemen stationed in London: "Although an untrained nobody a few months before, [he] saved London from destruction, and by so doing, saved the world. For, make no mistake about it, the real crisis of the war came on the night of Saturday, September 7, 1940." Swaffer in his text celebrates the heroism of one particular fireman, Jack Maynard, his nominee for the "Unknown Civilian," and his "mates" on the Beckenham pump crew, "Ginger" Beckham, "Taxi" Udders, Dave Chalmers, and Carl Taylor. As Swaffer informs us, all but one of these firemen died.[28]

The memories of two men who worked closely with the firemen provide a vivid picture of what happened after the fire. W. B. Regan and Bert Freeman, members of the Heavy Rescue Service in Poplar, were off duty but reported to their depot when the raid started on September 7. All of the firemen were gone to "incidents." A call came for help, so the two of them went and assisted with digging out a building whose brickwork had, in Regan's words, "simply fragmented and collapsed into a heap of fire rubble." They had little hope of finding survivors, and indeed, at dawn as the All Clear was sounding, the pair uncovered a corpse:

> He was an elderly man, fully dressed, and still sitting in his armchair, but totally embedded in fine plaster, and brick rubble. We could not lift him out, until we had freed him entirely, the stuff was packed almost solid around him. We rescued the armchair undamaged. ... We got our bicycles at the end of the road where we had left them and came away about 7.00 A.M. ... Had a cup of tea and to the depot for my 24 hour shift. Out at 8.30 A.M. Canton St. and took over from A. shift. Landscape re-arranged, and beginning to look like Spain and Poland. ... The school playground shed had been screened off for the cleaning and shrouding [of the dead]; I never saw them coffined. It was fine, warm weather, and the shed was wide open, with the bodies lying on the asphalt; [the member of the mortuary staff] soon, by order and example, had his men stripping off what clothing remained on the corpses. "Now wash 'em off" he says, and the first one to try, had a water-bucket and a sponge, and began to gently wash the face of one corpse with a sponge. The expert soon stopped that; he wasn't going to have a four hour job. He ordered two of his men to keep the buckets of water coming, and with a

> long-handled, well wetted mop, gave the first corpse a good wash, back and front, showed his men how to wrap them in shrouds, label them, and stow them for final disposal. Each one took about 3 to 4 minutes, and as he said, "that's how it's done, you'll get the hang of it soon enough." I don't think they ever did.

Regan continued to work until Monday morning, doing some firefighting, but mainly trying to rescue people. On Monday morning, at 8 a.m. "when I got home I found Vi was alright and Jackie Bowers and his wife, who had been in the Anderson with her. The rest of our windows had gone, so I spent some time helping Vi to tidy up. Went along to her Mum and Dad and had a chin-wag, and he asked me if I had managed to get any sleep, and when we reckoned it up, I found I had none for about 76 hours." He spent that night, Monday, in the family's Anderson shelter. "Three bombs, in quick succession, just like close, closer, and we both thought curtains, when the last one came, but it was near, and only shook us up, then a rattling of falling bricks and tiles. We didn't bother much after this, and we lay on our bunks and drank tea from our flask, and talked about our two children, trying to decide what to get for their Christmas presents."[29]

The special horror of the bombing was emphasized by Ritchie Calder, a journalist and activist. He noted how one fireman, a veteran of the First World War, viewed the difference between then and now: "You grow wise to a shell-barrage ... but there's no getting wise to bombs. And there we were bang in the middle of a lighted target!" Calder continued, "It was the fires which made that first day and night of the Blitzkrieg seem the worst of all the raids. Other great fires were to follow during subsequent weeks, but not with the same cumulative violence."[30]

VI

Picking up the Pieces

"It almost broke our hearts"

ONCE the All Clear had sounded on Sunday morning, September 8, Londoners stumbled out of their shelters and looked at a world transformed. The reactions – from ordinary citizens to members of the press, the government and the military – were as varied as humanity itself. Some people were panicked and despairing; others maintained a "stiff upper lip" and vowed to carry on as before.

The scene that greeted them was surreal. As one resident remembered: "The next morning, in a state of shock we took a walk round the houses. It was as though there had been an earthquake. Beds were hanging from bedroom floors, broken glass, bricks, rubble and thick dust everywhere. There was a funny sort of quietness, almost as though you were in another world, not real."[1]

Warden Barbara Nixon captured how everything was now different.

> At dawn the "all clear" went, and groups of pale and jaded people trailed back to their homes to snatch a cup of tea before leaving for work. ... All the rumours of war, and the

> warnings of aerial bombardment of the last five years, all the bombing of the Spanish towns, the destruction of Warsaw and Rotterdam, had not made them pause to think what it might be like when it came to them, and they were shocked and stunned. That day London had changed. … At last people realised that there was a serious war on – a war that meant visible death and destruction, not only newspaper articles and recruiting posters and war memorials. And they did not like the realisation. … The British public had not had any training, physical or moral, to help it to withstand the nervous strain of being bombed.[2]

In East Ham, Gladys Streilitz and her family had spent the night in a church. She reported, "As we got out of the crypt, we could see the Home Guard actually digging out bodies. And the smouldering flames and the stench was terrible and the sky was all lit up with flames." Shaken, Gladys and her family left London for Maidenhead.[3]

In middle-class Eltham, Bill Snellgrove had remained up all night in the garden reading by the light of the distant flames. When he got up at midday, he saw

> a large double decker bus outside. … Clambering out of the bus were refugees, the sort we've only seen on newsreels. … They were the homeless from North Woolwich. Some had battered old cases, some had bundles of clothing and other belongings. A few seemed cheerful but most of them were silent, sad or crying. But they all had a dazed, dusty look which I shall never forget. … All of them were starving hungry, so mum and Mrs Collins made them tea and took over biscuits as well and any other food they could rake up.[4]

The BBC was understated in its account broadcast on the Sunday morning news. That it was the largest raid so far was acknowledged, but the destruction was minimized. "Some damage has been caused to docks, residential areas and industrial premises. So far as is known at present three churches and two hospitals, including a children's nursing home, have been damaged."[5]

The reports in the press and on the radio did not underplay the seriousness of the situation, but they tended to put a positive spin on matters in order to soft-pedal the raids' grimmer aspects. The headline of one Sunday paper, the *People*, read "Biggest Daylight Raid of War Beaten Off," as if Britain had already won the air battle. Its stories emphasized how thousands at two football games and one greyhound race course stayed put and watched the aerial dogfights taking place above them, almost as if they were at another sporting event. Bombs did fall on the 6,000 people at the greyhound track but apparently no one was hurt and only one dog ran away. The story in the *Sunday Express* on September 8 ended, "There is no reason whatsoever for dejection or depression. The R.A.F. is more than holding its own."

The Times did not publish on Sundays, so its coverage of the raid appeared on Monday, September 9. Its news stories emphasized that this was the heaviest raid yet, but it too dwelt on the positive aspects. *The Times* reported that 99 German planes were downed. This was an exaggeration. In fact, the figures for both raids of September 7 were 63 German planes – 33 bombers and 30 fighters – destroyed or damaged in various ways, mostly by RAF action. In the second raid only one German aircraft was shot down, and that by an anti-aircraft gun.[6] (There was very little defensive anti-aircraft fire because half of the guns had been moved elsewhere to try to cope with German attacks on air bases around the country. On September 7, there were only 264 anti-aircraft guns in London, but within two days the number was doubled.[7]) Another defensive measure, barrage balloons – large floating dirigible objects designed to hinder the bombers from coming too low and to make observation from above more difficult – were also of some help. In this first major raid, the Luftwaffe brought down 27 RAF fighters and two more were missing; about a dozen more were damaged. Fourteen British pilots lost their lives.[8]

The Times did admit that there was "severe and widespread damage" and many casualties. Somewhat as an excuse, the paper pointed out that the RAF had been busy bombing harbours in France in order to lessen the threat of invasion. (During September, the RAF made 3,000 bombing raids on enemy targets.)[9] In fact, British fighters hardly engaged with the Germans the first day of the Blitz, presumably since they did not have the strength of numbers to do so and experienced greater difficulty attacking by night.

The canonical paper of record acknowledged the seriousness of the September 7 raid:

> The attacks were concentrated on the thickly populated riverside area East of the City, and it is provisionally estimated that about 400 people have been killed and some 1,300 to 1,400 seriously injured. ... They started out as raids on military and other legitimate targets, but towards the end they degenerated into indiscriminate bombing with the result that hundreds of civilians were killed and injured, even greater numbers rendered homeless, and fairly widespread damage caused. ... The raids were described as a reprisal for R.A.F. attacks on Berlin. They are, of course, in no way comparable. Our bombers have attacked only selected military targets; much of the London raids appeared to have but a "terror" purpose.

6. Winston Churchill was at Chequers during the first wave of attacks, but returned to London to tour the devastated East End on September 8, 1940.

Winston Churchill, the Prime Minister, was at his official country residence, Chequers, over the weekend, but he'd been kept abreast of events. He returned on Sunday afternoon, when he toured the East End to see the extent of the damage. Meanwhile, the government issued an upbeat, rather unclear, and quite untrue statement, which appeared in *The Times* and elsewhere the next day: "Damage was severe but judged against the background of the war is not serious." To a modern eye, the word "background" looks very ambiguous. As we shall see, there was much chaos and inadequacy on the part of government agencies that was conspicuously not part of the newspapers' reports. The official statement continued:

> A number of persons were rendered temporarily homeless, but were successfully removed from the danger area and

> immediate steps were taken to provide them with food and shelter. … Through all these areas the civil defence services are speedily and successfully dealing with the tasks imposed upon them. … As was expected, there is evidence from all areas of the high courage and resolution with which the civil population have accepted this challenge.

The Times editorial that day continued the theme of terror: "The enemy undoubtedly endeavoured to deliver a crushing blow in the spirit of his policy of terrorization." The rest of the piece was to a degree whistling in the dark, although the claim that the raid was a failure because of the enemy's losses of planes had some validity. Also it was true that the two further purposes of the raid – the destruction of docks, shipping, factories, and communications and the destruction of morale – had failed, even if both the tangible and intangible constituents that made up London had certainly been seriously battered. As had Churchill, *The Times* visited the East End on Sunday. "These people had been through a terrible experience. Many had had narrow escapes. Many were homeless. But their general verdict was that the endurance was an incident in the process of winning the war over a ruthless enemy; and that they were not going to flinch until the mastery was won." Reports were given of the destruction in London of schools, churches, a shelter and hospital wards, but so as not to provide the enemy with specifics no exact names or locations were given.

The Times continued its traditions despite the war. The editorial page had its famous light-hearted "fourth leader," this time a disquisition, "Cockney Welsh," on the odd situation of evacuated London children learning Welsh. The photographs that day showed a bombed church and school but, following government policy, without their location. There was also a picture of a downed

German raider. A further news story dwelt on the German failure to carry out a second Rotterdam – that is, a raid that would cause a wish to surrender.

The *Daily Express* belonged to Lord Beaverbrook. Pugnacious and powerful, he had entered the government when Churchill became Prime Minister as Minister of Air Production and later Minister of Supply. In August, he became one of the six members of the War Cabinet. The *Express* noted with patriotic exaggeration:

> So the great blitz of London has started. ... Thrashed and beaten in daylight battle, having no more hope of military success against us in the air, Goering thinks he can shake us by terrorism as he first cowed his own people. To smash the British Empire he picks the weakest, poorest and most defenceless of our population found in some of the meanest streets of the East End of London. ... He smashes poor Jewish households, little Cockney homes. What a piece of dirty brutality in plan and in deed. As warfare it will not work. It will merely fan the flame of righteous hate in every British heart. ... So civilian and soldier alike we will gird ourselves with new determination to wage the war.

Surprisingly, the paper ran as a straightforward news story the German claims for victory over London; the Nazi propaganda machine asserted that the Underground had been destroyed and the overall damage was "incalculable." Perhaps because these claims were visibly not true, it was valuable for the *Daily Express* to publish the story. Photographs showed bombing damage, as well as women and children with prams full of their belongings, seeking refuge. As Hilde Marchant's lead story began, "The civilian population is taking its Dunkirk." It was a very apt comparison. Both events, one military, the other civilian, were seeming defeats that became transformed into both understated and in some sense glorious psychological victories. She emphasized, with understandable optimism, how the bombed-out poor were looking for new places to establish themselves. On the back page of the paper, where the story continued, there was an advertisement that also recommended a way to preserve equanimity: "No Act of Parliament compels you to look after yourself. It's up to you. The first and most important step is to keep your bowels open and your kidneys well flushed. Kruschen does this for you in the simplest possible way."[10]

What was new on Sunday, September 8, and the following week – especially as the Luftwaffe returned each night to bomb London – was a sense that a German invasion was a very real possibility. That the highest command thought that invasion was extremely likely to happen in these few days is made vividly clear in the diary of Alan Brooke, commander-in-chief of the Home Forces and later (1941) to become Chief of the Imperial General Staff. In the context of possible invasion, the air raid of September 7 could easily be seen as the prelude. Brooke had had dinner with Churchill at Chequers that Friday night, and on Saturday came to London. "All reports look like invasion getting nearer. Ships collecting, dive bombers being concentrated, parachutists captured [?], also 4 Dutchmen [spies] on the coast."[11] This prediction was based on photographic reconnaissance recording that the Germans were gathering numerous barges, presumably for the transport of troops, at various Channel ports.

On September 8, Brooke wrote: "Heavy bombing of London throughout the night, the whole sky being lit up by the glow of fires in London docks. Went to the office in the morning where I found further indications of impending invasion." He had lunch that day with his family outside London before returning in the evening. "It seemed so strange leaving you [his diary was addressed to his wife] and all the peace and happiness connected with our combined lives to return here for what may well be the most eventful weeks in the history of the British Empire! ... All reports still point to the probability of an invasion starting between the 8th and the 10th of this month." These would be propitious days in terms of a full moon and high tides. When commenting on this passage later in the 1950s, he wrote:

> I do not think I can remember any time in the whole of my career when my responsibilities weighed heavier on me than they did during those days of the impending invasion. The full knowledge of all that depended on my preparations for, and conduct of, the battle to repel the invasion, combined with the unpleasant realization as to the deficiencies of equipment and training in the forces at my disposal, made the prospect of the impending conflict a burden that was almost unbearable at times.

With many exceptions of course, at all levels of society there was a great emphasis on not showing fear, on rising above the situation, on conforming, one might say, to the stereotype of the British character of the "stiff upper lip." In that respect, Brooke's retrospective analysis of early September is illuminating for, added to the burdens of government, he says, "was the necessity to maintain outward confident appearance, there was not a soul to whom one could disclose one's inward anxieties without risking the calamitous effects of lack of confidence, demoralization, doubts, and all those insidious workings which undermine the power of resistance." This comment suggests, I think, a major psychological reason why the British were able to survive these days of crisis, as well as the ongoing days of the Blitz. As well, compared to many other nations, despite many bureaucratic failures, Britain had a powerful infrastructure. Class-ridden as it may have been, it was a democratic state in which many, whether in opposition or support, were involved in the political process.

On Saturday, before the first raid had begun, the Chiefs of Staff had met in London and the Director of Military Intelligence, F. G. Beaumont-Nesbitt, informed them that invasion might be imminent, perhaps on Sunday, September 8. The Chiefs of Staff considered sending out the code term "Cromwell," indicating an invasion was about to be launched. Once the German air attack started, Brigadier John Swayne did send out such an alert, at 8:07 p.m., to the London, Southern and Eastern Army commands. It remained in effect for 12 days.[12] The "Cromwell" warning was ambiguous: it was meant to signify that the units should prepare for invasion. But quite a few interpreted it as indicating that the invasion had actually started. Rumours were rife and many reported, particularly along the south coast, seeing German troops. Some Home Guard commanders ordered that church bells be rung, even though they were only to be employed for an actual invasion by parachutists. They were sounded in towns ranging from Portsmouth to Swansea, alerting a half-million members of the Home Guard.[13] The belief held by some – reinforced by rampant rumours that were going around – that the country was actually being invaded increased the sense of panic.

Consider the advice issued over Churchill's name, entitled: "Beating the INVADER." Harold Nicolson and Sir Kenneth Clark, the Director of the National Gallery, as members of the Home Morale Emergency Committee of the Ministry of Information, had drafted

Issued by the Ministry of Information  *in co-operation with the War Office and the Ministry of Home Security*

Beating the INVADER

A MESSAGE FROM THE PRIME MINISTER

If invasion comes, everyone—young or old, men and women—will be eager to play their part worthily. By far the greater part of the country will not be immediately involved. Even along our coasts, the greater part will remain unaffected. But where the enemy lands, or tries to land, there will be most violent fighting. Not only will there be the battles when the enemy tries to come ashore, but afterwards there will fall upon his lodgments very heavy British counter-attacks, and all the time the lodgments will be under the heaviest attack by British bombers. The fewer civilians or non-combatants in these areas, the better—apart from essential workers who must remain. So if you are advised by the authorities to leave the place where you live, it is your duty to go elsewhere when you are told to leave. When the attack begins, it will be too late to go; and, unless you receive definite instructions to move, your duty then will be to stay where you are. You will have to get into the safest place you can find, and stay there until the battle is over. For all of you then the order and the duty will be: "STAND FIRM".

This also applies to people inland if any considerable number of parachutists or air-borne troops are landed in their neighbourhood. Above all, they must not cumber the roads. Like their fellow-countrymen on the coasts, they must "STAND FIRM". The Home Guard, supported by strong mobile columns wherever the enemy's numbers require it, will immediately come to grips with the invaders, and there is little doubt will soon destroy them.

Throughout the rest of the country where there is no fighting going on and no close cannon fire or rifle fire can be heard, everyone will govern his conduct by the second great order and duty, namely, "CARRY ON". It may easily be some weeks before the invader has been totally destroyed, that is to say, killed or captured to the last man who has landed on our shores. Meanwhile, all work must be continued to the utmost, and no time lost.

The following notes have been prepared to tell everyone in rather more detail what to do, and they should be carefully studied. Each man and woman should think out a clear plan of personal action in accordance with the general scheme.

Winston S. Churchill

STAND FIRM

1. What do I do if fighting breaks out in my neighbourhood?

Keep indoors or in your shelter until the battle is over. If you can have a trench ready in your garden or field, so much the better. You may want to use it for protection if your house is damaged. But if you are at work, or if you have special orders, carry on as long as possible and only take cover when danger approaches. If you are on your way to work, finish your journey if you can.

If you see an enemy tank, or a few enemy soldiers, do not assume that the enemy are in control of the area. What you have seen may be a party sent on in advance, or stragglers from the main body who can easily be rounded up.

7. A wartime message issued by the Ministry of Information to 46 million Britons.

it the previous June.[14] There was then quite an intense sense of the enemy within, of traitors and spies. There was a fear that Germans might be parachuted into the country disguised as Boy Scouts, nuns, clergymen, even as air raid wardens. With the war going badly, there

CARRY ON

2. What do I do in areas which are some way from the fighting?

Stay in your district and carry on. Go to work whether in shop, field, factory or office. Do your shopping, send your children to school until you are told not to. Do not try to go and live somewhere else. Do not use the roads for any unnecessary journey; they must be left free for troop movements even a long way from the district where actual fighting is taking place.

3. Will certain roads and railways be reserved for the use of the Military, even in areas far from the scene of action?

Yes, certain roads will have to be reserved for important troop movements; but such reservations should be only temporary. As far as possible, bus companies and railways will try to maintain essential public services, though it may be necessary to cut these down. Bicyclists and pedestrians may use the roads for journeys to work, unless instructed not to do so.

ADVICE AND ORDERS

4. Whom shall I ask for advice?

The police and A.R.P. wardens.

5. From whom shall I take orders?

In most cases from the police and A.R.P. wardens. But there may be times when you will have to take orders from the military and the Home Guard in uniform.

6. Is there any means by which I can tell that an order is a true order and not faked?

You will generally know your policeman and your A.R.P. wardens by sight, and can trust them. With a bit of common sense you can tell if a soldier is really British or only pretending to be so. If in doubt ask a policeman, or ask a soldier whom you know personally.

INSTRUCTIONS

7. What does it mean when the church bells are rung?

It is a warning to the local garrison that troops have been seen landing from the air in the neighbourhood of the church in question. Church bells will *not* be rung all over the country as a general warning that invasion has taken place. The ringing of church bells in one place will not be taken up in neighbouring churches.

8. Will instructions be given over the wireless?

Yes; so far as possible. But remember that the enemy can overhear any wireless message, so that the wireless cannot be used for instructions which might give him valuable information.

9. In what other ways will instructions be given?

Through the Press; by loudspeaker vans; and perhaps by leaflets and posters. But remember that genuine Government leaflets will be given to you only by the policeman, your A.R.P. warden or your postman; while genuine posters and instructions will be put up only on Ministry of Information notice boards and official sites, such as police stations, post offices, A.R.P. posts, town halls and schools.

FOOD

10. Should I try to lay in extra food?

No. If you have already laid in a stock of food, keep it for a real emergency; but do not add to it. The Government has made arrangements for food supplies.

NEWS

11. Will normal news services continue?

Yes. Careful plans have been made to enable newspapers and wireless broadcasts to carry on, and in case of need there are emergency measures which will bring you the news. But if there should be some temporary breakdown in news supply, it is very important that you should not listen to rumours nor pass them on, but should wait till real news comes through again. Do not use the telephones or send telegrams if you can possibly avoid it.

MOTOR-CARS

12. Should I put my car, lorry or motor-bicycle out of action?

Yes, when you are told to do so by the police, A.R.P. wardens or military; or when it is obvious that there is an immediate risk of its being seized by the enemy—then disable and hide your bicycle and destroy your maps.

13. How should it be put out of action?

Remove distributor head and leads and either empty the tank or remove the carburettor. If you don't know how to do this, find out now from your nearest garage. In the case of diesel engines remove the injection pump and connection. The parts removed must be hidden well away from the vehicle.

THE ENEMY

14. Should I defend myself against the enemy?

The enemy is not likely to turn aside to attack separate houses. If small parties are going about threatening persons and property in an area not under enemy control and come your way, you have the right of every man and woman to do what you can to protect yourself, your family and your home.

GIVE ALL THE HELP YOU CAN TO OUR TROOPS

Do not tell the enemy anything

Do not give him anything

Do not help him in any way

(S506) Wt. 46581/F1609 14,050,800 (2 kds.) 6/41 Hw. G.51

was an almost excessive fear of defeatism. Those in authority tended to underestimate the morale of the working class.[15] At the same time, this attitude at times alternated with a belief that the people would "cope." Neither attitude was based on much hard knowledge.

Churchill and his War Cabinet met at midday on Monday together with various other members of the Cabinet and military advisers. According to the terse minutes of the meeting, the air raids were not the only (or even the primary) topic, though note was taken of how much damage had been done to the railways, the docks and local hospitals. Instead the meeting focused on the maintenance of the war effort, including establishing a system of watchers or spotters on the roofs of factories, allowing production to continue until attack was imminent. The preparations for possible invasion were going forward, with a report that 60 per cent of the population had been evacuated already from 19 major towns along the east coast with more to follow. News of this development was to be kept out of the press.[16]

During the early months of Britain's war, one of Churchill's most important aims was to secure as much American support as possible. A major component of this was the American reporters and broadcasters who were already in London covering the conflict, the most famous being Edward R. Murrow. On the whole they were very pro-British (in contrast to the American ambassador, Joseph Kennedy, who did not believe that the British could stand up to the Germans). About a hundred American reporters were in London, including Quentin Reynolds, who narrated *London Can Take It*, Humphrey Jennings's brilliant short film made as part of the effort to persuade the Americans to support Britain. Among the others were Eric Sevareid, Negley Farson, John Gunther, James (Scotty) Reston, and Ben Robertson.[17]

As it so happened, Ben Robertson spent September 7 with Ed Murrow and Vincent Sheean, a roving reporter who had worked for the *Chicago Tribune*. In his telegram to *PM* that day, Robertson reported – and he thought people in Britain shared this view – that the RAF would hold out against the pounding it was receiving from the Luftwaffe. He also surmised that the pessimistic American ambassador was finally coming around: "Even Joe Kennedy is feeling better today," he reported, having talked to the ambassador that morning.

Partly because Robertson had thought that a major attack might take place that Saturday, the three American reporters decided to drive to the east of London in order to have a better view. (During the Battle of Britain, they frequently had driven down to Dover on the coast to observe aerial dog-fights.) In Murrow's Sunbeam Talbot, they travelled through Limehouse and Stepney, noting ordinary life going on as people bought food for their Sunday dinners. "We watched seven big ships moving up the Thames, steaming closely toward London," Robertson wrote. "Then we crossed over the river, bought three tin-hatfuls of apples from a farmer for two shillings, and coming on a haystack on the edge of a turnip-field, we lay down to eat apples and to sleep in the sun."

Then the first air raid began, and Robertson, Murrow, and Sheean were joined in a ditch by a bicycling boy and girl, and a busload of passengers. "Sheean, in the ditch, kept saying: 'This is just like Spain.'" They adjourned to a pub, and discussed with the proprietress the poor women and children in London. She was particularly worried about how animals would react to the raid.

> When night came, we went back to the haystack and watched the most appalling and depressing sight any of us had ever seen. We were horrified by the sight. It almost made us physically ill to see the enormity of the flames which lit the entire western sky. The London that we knew was burning – the London which had taken thirty generations of men a

> thousand years to build – and the Nazis had done that in thirty seconds. ... The night was like the Revelation of St. John. It almost broke our hearts to think of what the world had to lose in that city. ... Finally we drove to a hotel in Gravesend and slept in our clothes.

The next day they drove back to the centre of London, going through the East End.

> We saw factories gutted and docks burning and bomb craters. ... That was a depressing sight, but what really disturbed us was the East End itself. We saw English men and women, standing in streets with all they had in suitcases, waiting to be evacuated. ... All along the way we had passed so quietly the day before, we now saw destruction. ... The Battle of London had started, and on that first Sunday it seemed to all of us like the end of civilization.[18]

Ed Murrow made the same trip the topic for his radio broadcast from London on Sunday night. "Yesterday afternoon – it seems days ago now – I drove down to the East End of London, the East India Dock Road, Commercial Road, through Silvertown, down to the mouth of the Thames Estuary. It was a quiet and almost pleasant trip through those streets running between rows of working-class houses, with the cranes, the docks, the ships, and the oil tanks off on the right." His broadcast mostly emphasized the efforts of the British fighters against the bombers. He too mentioned the visit to the pub where the Americans had dinner. "Children were already organizing a hunt for bits of shrapnel. Under some bushes beside the road there was a baker's cart. Two boys, still sobbing, were trying to get a quivering bay mare back between the shafts. The lady who

8. From September 7 onwards, the bombing of civilian targets became a matter of German policy. Here the previous night's bombing ripped apart a block of dwellings, exposing the crowded conditions of working-class life. East London, September 9, 1940.

ran the pub told us that these raids were bad for the chickens, the dogs, and the horses."

They returned to the haystack and

> the fires up the river had turned the moon blood red. The smoke had drifted till it formed a canopy over the Thames.

> … Vincent Sheean lay on one side of me and cursed in five languages. … Ben Robertson, of *PM*, lay on the other side and kept saying over and over in that slow South Carolina drawl, "London is burning, London is burning." … This afternoon we drove back to the East End of London. It was like an obstacle race – two blocks to the right, then left for four blocks, then straight on for a few blocks, and right again. … Three red buses drawn up in a line waiting to take the homeless away. … There was still fire and smoke along the river, but the fire fighters and the demolition squads have done their work well.

The next night, September 9, Murrow broadcast again and wondered what the point of the bombing was. "This night bombing is serious and sensational. It makes headlines, kills people, and smashes property; but it doesn't win wars." He ventured to guess that "the Germans know that, know that several days of terror bombing will not cause the country to collapse."[19] The Germans may well have had serious hopes that the heavy raids that initial weekend might lead the British government to move toward a negotiated peace.

Vincent Sheean, the third member of this American trio, also wrote about September 7. Drawing on his Spanish Civil War experience, he was very grateful for a ditch to be in while observing the raid. There was, according to him and contrary to some accounts of the day, quite a bit of anti-aircraft fire; however, the three reporters might have been near air bases where the guns had been moved. They observed the vast fires of the oil tanks at Thameshaven. After dinner, they returned to the ditch and the haystack to watch the second raid. With it, the flames became more and more intense. "The monstrous inferno before us was like nothing I or anybody else in this century had ever seen. … It was like a vision of the end of the world." Sheean had a sense of the English past hurling itself into the flames. "Wat Tyler and John Lackland, Edward the Black Prince and Will Shakespeare, Nelson and Fair Rosamond, all the song and all the story, now to be burnt out. … Who could convince them [the Germans] that the fire they set this night would consume them, too, before it was quenched?" They went to the inn at Gravesend, where Sheean slept well, despite the raid and the light. But he did have a nightmare about a German invasion of the United States. On the trip back to London, he recorded, as had his colleagues, the destruction and the people "like the poor in all wars, taking to the road. They did it, however, in a patient and orderly way, their faces a little stunned, a little shocked."[20]

Another conduit of information to the United States was the English writer Mollie Panter-Downes, who wrote her "Letter from London" for the *New Yorker.* In a column dated September 8, she emphasized the terror aspect of the bombing as deliberately targeting working-class districts. She did not even mention that it had hit the area of the docks. Although she put it in spatial terms, Panter-Downes took a rather patronizing attitude toward the poor, suggesting that working-class districts were "structurally more vulnerable and emotionally more prone to panic than less crowded areas of a city." That was contrasted to "those who were weekending in the country [who] guessed the magnitude of the attack from the constant roar of aircraft passing invisibly high up in the cloudless blue sky. … This morning it was difficult to get a call through to London, probably because so many anxious people in the country were ringing up to find out what had happened and to try to get in touch with members of their families who were in town."[21]

In the Edward R. Murrow papers at Tufts University, there is an undated manuscript, presumably of a broadcast. It was probably delivered some days later, as its theme is the underground shelters in the London tube. It is perhaps a somewhat romanticized picture, but yet again it illustrates the crucial importance at the time of not appearing to be afraid. Murrow wrote,

> Not all of them are heroes. Sometimes they will scream and surge to one side of the shelter when a big bomb comes roaring down. But the thing that is important is that they down their fears and come up smiling; come up out of those holes in the ground with the sticky, damp odour of human sweat and often-breathed air still clinging to them. ... They are sustained by the history, tradition and folk-lore of this island; supported by that well-mannered sub-surface British arrogance which admits no questioning of the superiority of Britain and Britishers over any and all other nations and other peoples.[22]

After the first night of bombing in the East End, the South Hallsville School in Canning Town was full of refugees. Located on Agate Street just north of Victoria Dock, the school now hosted homeless from Silvertown and the Tidal Basin. These areas were within the London borough of West Ham, but its Council did not have a shelter to which it could send them. The bombing of this school on the third night of the Blitz, September 9–10, has been the focus of much subsequent attention.

On Sunday, Ritchie Calder, the writer, who was also a member of the Labour Party's committee on air raid precautions, went to the East End and met up with a friend, W. W. Paton, a Presbyterian minister whose church had been destroyed. The two men went to the nearby South Hallsville School, where many of the homeless were sheltering. It became the central point of Calder's 1941 *The Lesson of London*.[23] "In the passages and the classrooms were mothers nursing their babies. There were blind, crippled, and aged people," Calder reported. "Whole families were sitting in queues, perched on their pitiful baggage, waiting desperately for coaches to take them away from the terror of the bombs. ... The crowded people in the school included many families who had been bombed out already, on that first night. These unfortunate homeless people had been told to be ready for the coaches at three o'clock." As the afternoon passed, the promised buses did not arrive, and the local residents in the shelter badgered officials for more information; according to Calder, "the harassed officials knew no answer other than the offer of a cup of tea." (This is eerily similar to the aftermath of Hurricane Katrina in 2005, when buses intended to evacuate residents from "shelters of last resort" at the Superdome in New Orleans and the city's convention center took days to arrive.)

Calder considered the school "a bulging, dangerous ruin" – in fact, it had been somewhat damaged in the first night's raid. He had a strong sense then and there that the school would be a target again. (He writes, "It was not a premonition. It was a calculable certainty.") Nevertheless, during his visit, he was impressed by the resilience of the East Enders. Emblematic was a child who had managed to sleep through the crash of a bomb seven yards away. He was now careening in and out of rooms and the yard, pretending to be a Spitfire. Calder compared such children to the recovering soldiers he had seen after Dunkirk, and how both had been cured by sleep. Again, the situation emphasized the similarities between what soldiers and civilians were enduring. In his science column in the *New Statesman*, Calder pointed out the necessity of sleep, and that people will learn how to sleep anyway, no matter how badly the Germans might bomb.[24]

Sleep deprivation was in fact a major problem. One nurse wrote in a letter to her husband on September 10: "The last three nights have been absolute hell! . . . I have not had more than 2 or 3 hours sleep on either night & I sleep in the afternoon whenever I can."[25]

Calder went from South Hallsville back to central London and warned authorities at Whitehall three times about the school's vulnerability. Simultaneously, Canning Town officials were repeatedly asked to get people away from the building before it was too late. On Monday, after all the evacuees had spent a second night huddled in the building, some were taken away – but this was done to make room for people made newly homeless in the Sunday night raids. According to a later inquiry, buses for evacuating the school had indeed been ordered on Sunday. The drivers were supposed to rendezvous at a nearby public house, but the instructions got garbled and instead of meeting in Canning Town, the buses went to Camden Town. In any event, they did not get to South Hallsville School until late on Monday. While the homeless were boarding them, the sirens sounded and it was decided to abandon the transfer that day, postponing it until the following day.

On Monday night, the school was still full as darkness fell, and at 3:45 a.m. a German bomb fell on the South Hallsville School, demolishing half the building.[26] Calder and others blamed the tragedy on "official blundering," and in *The Lesson of London*, he used this incident to lament the lost years of opportunities.

> After years of "preparation," the Government was unprepared for dealing with human problems. On the other hand, the personnel of the Civil Defence Services proved their worth. The tragedy of that East London school underlined the

9. 'A bulging, dangerous ruin': South Hallsville School reduced to rubble after being directly hit by a bomb on the third night of the Blitz. The deaths of the 'ordinary' people sheltering inside exposed the doleful inadequacy of official arrangements.

> unpreparedness. It is not sufficient excuse to blame the coach leader. The local authorities had a lot to answer for. So had the Government.[27]

It was, according to some, the biggest single civilian disaster of the war.[28]

Even when the coaches arrived to take off those who had survived the bombing of the school, the arrangements were unsatisfactory. One survivor, R. J. Rice, remembered in 1985: "Next morning, by virtue of pressure by the people, we were taken by London Transport buses to I don't think anyone knew where. We stopped on the Wanstead Flats during an air raid, spent two days at the Majestic Cinema, Woodford, a week in a church in Hoe Street, Walthamstow, and finally were taken to Finchley and housed in empty requisitioned houses."[29]

Through this and other failures, Calder reached a conclusion – the need for revolutionary change – similar to one that George Orwell had arrived at in *The Lion and the Unicorn*. Calder did not necessarily think that society would have to be transformed immediately, as Orwell did. But he felt that the extent of how "ordinary" people had suffered and the failure of those in authority to cope meant that eventually there would have to be a very different sort of world. Indeed, as he pointed out, the government recognized the need to take some action acknowledging its failure to prepare properly. John Anderson, an independent Member of Parliament, more of a civil servant than a politician, was replaced as Home Secretary by Herbert Morrison, the popular Labour leader who was deeply identified with London. Calder wrote in concluding his book, "In the perspective of history, the Lesson of London may be that 'Black Saturday', September 7th, 1940 was as significant in its own way – as Bastille Day, July 14th, 1789."[30]

The Times did not hide the tragedy of the bombing of South Hallsville School, although in line with government policy, no exact location was given.

> Many bodies have been recovered from a school in East London which was wrecked by a direct hit. Some of the persons extricated from beneath the mass of twisted girders and débris were still alive but died on the way to hospital. It is feared that there will be only a few survivors. The rescue squads found alive two babies, one aged nine months and the other six months. They were taken to hospital, and it is thought that they may recover. A tragic feature is that arrangements had been made for these refugees to be transferred to the country yesterday.[31]

The Home Intelligence Report, an in-house circular at the Ministry of Information, didn't hide the horror of the event.* On September 10 it stated: "Extreme nervousness of people rendered homeless at being herded together in local schools with inadequate shelters. West Ham school filled to bursting point from Saturday night onwards blown up by H[igh].E[xplosive] bomb with many casualties. This has caused great shock in the district."

The episode of the school has resurfaced at least twice quite recently. It formed a central causative event, although not depicted, in a recent episode, "The Funk Hole," of the British TV series *Foyle's War.* Foyle is a police detective in Hastings on the coast. The series has a fairly cynical attitude toward the war. This story begins with a young man, full of defeatism, ranting in an air-raid shelter. He has been somewhat unhinged by the rest of his family being killed in a bombing. Another element in the plot is a group of well-off Londoners who have sought refuge in a country hotel near Hastings. One of their number turns out to be the civil servant responsible for the mistake about the coaches that were to come

* These were first issued on May 18, 1940, and appeared daily until September 25; thereafter they were issued weekly until December 29, 1944. The Reports were labelled "Secret" and were intended for internal distribution and for relevant members of the government and civil service. Their existence, however, was known to the public, and some regarded them as being overly intrusive. The Minister of Information, Duff Cooper, wrote about the Intelligence Reports, "A number of carefully selected people had been charged by the Ministry of Information with the duty of studying the state of public opinion and reporting on the kind of criticism that was being made of the authorities. … I could claim no credit in the matter, as it had been set going before I became Minister, but now I had to bear the whole brunt of its misrepresentation. It was alleged that I had instituted a system of espionage which gave certain people the right to pry into the affairs of their neighbours, and 'Down with Cooper's Snoopers' became a slogan of the popular press" (Duff Cooper, *Old Men Forget* [London, 1953], pp. 286–7).

to the school. The mother and sister of a high-ranking London police officer were at the school and were killed because of the civil servant's incompetence. They were serving as volunteers in order to help with the East Enders who were sheltering there. Rather improbably, the police officer has worked out an elaborate plot to murder the civil servant, which indeed happens on the television show. But although the details are not convincing, I believe the plot of the episode in essence reveals something of the lasting power of the tragedy at the school in the consciousness of the British public.

Even more striking is Glyn Maxwell's book of poems *The Sugar Mile* (2005). It emphasizes the similarities of 9/11 to the London Blitz, particularly its first day. The title refers to the sugar from the Tate & Lyle warehouses burning on the Thames. Maxwell is an Englishman, born in 1962, who lives in New York. His book opens in a Manhattan bar at 86th Street and Broadway on Saturday, September 8, 2001. The protagonists in the connected series of poems are two Englishmen, one younger, Clint, and one older, Joe, and the bartender, Raul, who is about to leave this job to start work, on Monday, at the Windows on the World restaurant in the Twin Towers. The implication is that he will be killed there.

Most of the book is devoted to Joe's reminiscences of the first few days of the Blitz. He is a half-Italian paper boy, who delivers newspapers in the East End; among his customers is the Pray family. Joe and others are sheltering in the South Hallsville School on Agate Street, awaiting the coaches that are to come at three in the afternoon on Sunday to take them away. The children in the Pray family romanticize the countryside where they think they will be evacuated. Joe's family, except for his grandmother, have all been killed. He leaves the school and goes to the Prays' house, destroyed by bombs, where he finds not hoped for hidden treasure but rather a Tate & Lyle ledger in which one of the daughters has written about him. On his way back to the school, he sees the coaches and guides them to the school, but it is too late. The drivers had thought that the destination was Camden Town rather than Canning Town:

> is Agate Street the next street the next street.
> But the driver's torn apart and there's no next street.
>
> for all there is a castle wall of fire
> and howling there
>
> a frame
> and a fireman like a stickman taking aim
>
> his white
> jet
>
> turned to steam
> in no time.[32]

The tragedy at the school took on symbolic importance as an event that shouldn't have happened. It stood for the necessity of planning for a better state in the future in which the needs of all would be considered. The authorities were least well prepared for dealing with the homeless, most of whom they expected to be dead rather than needing help. There were inadequate medical services, inadequate feeding arrangements, particularly of hot food, there were no clothes or bedding. The designated agency was the one for public assistance, the descendant of the Poor Law authority. These were not the sorts of problem, nor on a scale that the agency was accustomed to deal with. Nor were the homeless those who were destitute, though undoubtedly poor. There had been a year or more to prepare and the authorities had failed miserably. The social critic Vera Brittain suggested at the time that the problems were so vast that only the central government could handle them. She felt as if she were living in the world of H. G. Wells's *The Shape of Things to Come*. She commented in a personal pacifist newsletter she produced during the war, "Well, this is war as Madrid, Pekin and Helsinki had known it. For all the warnings that I used to issue at public meetings, I don't think I ever quite believed that it would come to London."[33]

That the authorities were unprepared was famously pointed out in Richard M. Titmuss's *Problems of Social Policy* (1950), his volume in the series of the official history of the Second World War. Titmuss's ideas formed a crucial part of the making of the British welfare state, the conception that the state needed to widen its social responsibilities not only in wartime but also in time of peace. In his chapter on "The Challenge of London's Homeless," Titmuss pointed out that the public assistance administrators in charge of the homeless had a mind-set that differentiated between the poor and the fortunate. The bombs effectively eliminated that difference but left unaffected how bureaucrats thought about those they were meant to help. There was a false assumption that bombed-out individuals would be able to make their own arrangements, despite the chaotic and deeply upsetting situation in which they found themselves.

Meanwhile, the national civil service had refused to allot enough money to prepare adequately and had a tendency to think in mind-numbingly minuscule ways. (For instance, it would only pay for blankets to be used for people who were lodged away from their home borough, as the local authorities were supposed to pay for blankets for their own. The reasoning was that if too many free blankets were distributed too many people would be tempted to stay too long in a rest centre!) As Titmuss wrote:

> Most of the early reports [of the not inconsiderable homeless already caused by the smaller raids] failed to show imagination about the social consequences of air attack. The first operational report to the Ministry on housing damage from enemy aircraft drily recorded that "no question of poor relief has so far arisen." This limited conception of the community's obligation to those involved in total war was the cause of much of the subsequent trouble.[34]

As Titmuss points out, when the storm broke on September 7,

> Rest centre accommodation of a rough kind was available but with little structural protection, with inadequate sanitation and few amenities. No provision was made for a stay beyond a few hours. Blankets were few and far between. ... There was no first aid equipment in the centres and, consistent with the history of the poor law, little information was available to guide to the right sources those who needed help.[35]

Little thinking had been devoted to more permanent accommodation; it was seen as only a last resort as the assumption was that the homeless would work it out on their own.[36] Titmuss is quite devastating in pointing out how ill-prepared the authorities were and the resulting degree of chaos. There was plenty of anger on the part of the public. Yet amazingly there was little panic. The government did succeed in changing its way of acting and thinking during the course of the war. By the end of 1941, the situation had been totally transformed, with the central government taking responsibility. To a greater extent than ever before, the government recognized its obligations to all its citizens. This would be a very important legacy for the future. Although the roots for this change stretched back long before the Second World War, the war was crucial in bringing these ideas and actions forward dramatically. The crisis – made so much more acute by September 7 – played a major, perhaps a decisive part in changing the nature of the British state.

F. R. Barry, at the time a Canon of Westminster and vicar of St John's, Smith Square, felt that there was a great danger of antiwar demonstrations after September 7. His account is a dramatic example of direct action by someone who felt entitled to take it. It sounds almost too good to be true.

> The first night was absolutely appalling. There were no air defences that counted. ... The dense population in the poorer districts ... had to sit it out, watching their homes destroyed, suffering terror, mutilation and death, without any adequate refuge or protection. ... Early next morning I rang up No. 10 and asked for an interview with Brendan Bracken [at that point Parliamentary Private Secretary to Churchill]. I told him that this simply would not do. The Government were responsible for these people. And I added that if this were allowed to go on there would be anti-war demonstrations which the Government might not be able to contain. Bracken sent me on to the Home Office, where I made the same speech with some embellishments, and the Under-secretary wrote it all down. The following night a number of naval guns were mounted on lorries and sent out into the streets. They were not of the slightest use against the bombers, but they made an enormous and most encouraging noise and at least helped people to believe that the powers-that-be had not abandoned them.[37]

As it turned out, there were no riots or demonstrations, nor demands for peace. But over the first weekend of the Blitz, I believe, the nerve and spirit of those in the East End came close to breaking. Those who fled removed a lot of the pressure. The homeless were also eventually moved and found somewhere to live. It took some time, but the government did step in and took serious actions to cope with the homeless and the destruction, rather than the comparatively trivial notions mentioned in its earlier reports.

Although a certain number of the working class fled the city, and quite a few children had been evacuated, the vast majority of working-class adults had no choice but to stay put. Many middle-class Londoners also had jobs that kept them in the city but those not working had a choice whether to leave or not. There was even a sense of differentiation between those who remained in London and those who commuted out of it daily. Graham Greene wrote in his wartime novel, *The Ministry of Fear*, "Through the blacked-out station the season-ticket holders were making a quick get-away from the nightly death; they dived in earnest silence towards the suburban trains, carrying little attaché-cases, and the porters stood and watched them go with an air of sceptical superiority. They felt the pride of being a legitimate objective: the pride of people who stayed."[38]

The government had quite miscalculated the effect of the first great air raid. The prediction had been that there would be many more deaths. Tragic as they would be, bodies – though presenting all sorts of difficulties – were nevertheless terminal problems. The homeless were not, and they were much harder to deal with. According to Caroline Lang's 1989 book *Keep Smiling Through*, 35 times as many civilians were made homeless as were killed. In all of Great Britain, over 2 million homes were destroyed by June 1941, with the figure rising to 3.5 million by the end of the war.[39]

As the three American reporters vividly remembered as they returned to London on September 8, the streets of the East End were full of the homeless. Some were just seeking shelter for the next night's raid. Some were displaced from their houses temporarily because their streets were closed by unexploded bombs. Some simply wished to leave the dangerous city. But many no longer had a home to go to. Some 5,000 trekked eastwards to Epping Forest and elsewhere in Essex. Many needed help to relocate, and the authorities were at first far from adequately prepared to deal with the situation. Where were the homeless to go and how were they to get there? They needed to be evacuated. (The tragedy of New Orleans has reminded us how serious this problem can be.) The numbers were overwhelming, and the hopes of the authorities that people would make their own arrangements were totally unrealistic. Earlier in the war, the evacuation of children had worked comparatively smoothly. Although there were all sorts of billeting problems at their destinations, such difficulties were generally resolved in a satisfactory manner. But that had not been an emergency situation and could proceed at its own pace. September 7 was a crisis, and it had not been correctly anticipated. Too much attention had been paid to the possibility of a gas attack and the likelihood of many thousands dead. The authorities had only a limited conception of their responsibilities to the homeless population, delegating the provision of services to peacetime agencies which had been designed to deal with the poverty-stricken and were likely to have patronizing assumptions and inadequate staff both in numbers and training.

As bombing continued in the weeks to come, the East Enders would not only trek further east into Essex but some would also travel to the West End, particularly Oxford Street, where they would seek shelter in the basements of its department stores. The West End's grand hotels were well known for providing luxurious shelter accommodation for their guests. There, some days later on September 15, a group of the poor, led by a few Communists, demanded shelter at the Savoy Hotel. By chance that day the raid was a short one, and the group docilely left immediately after the raid, after taking up a collection for the Savoy's staff, who had treated them well. This was one indication, I believe, that revolution was unlikely in Britain.

Meanwhile, the disastrous bureaucratic missteps were not hidden. The September issues of *Picture Post*, a weekly illustrated magazine of great popularity, reported the failures to deal with the problems caused by the Blitz (the same issue contained a positive and not totally accurate account of the success of British bombing of Germany, and the losses of German planes over Britain).

For instance, it quoted at length the experiences of a man from Stepney.

> "I been bombed out. That's my house, that heap of rubbish. I been 48 hours trying to get someone to do something about it. Can't get money, can't get my furniture out (what's left of it), I've only got the clothes I stand up in. I went to the Food Centre at the People's Palace – they hadn't got no grub. They sent me to the District Centre for Rationing down Barnes Street. They could do nothing. They sent me down East India Dock Road to the U.A.B. [Unemployment Assistance Board, representing the central government]. The U.A.B. told me it was a case for the P.A.C. [Public Assistance Committee, the local body], so I saw them, but no go. … I got fed up. Asked 'em if somebody couldn't make up their minds where I really ought to go. They ordered me out of the office, said

> they had enough of my sort coming in all day, demanding this and that. The neighbours gave me food – I have to rely on neighbours. It baffles you. When you do get bombed out, they rump you and tump you and buffer you about – and what's more, they're rude to you!"[40]

The homeless needed places to go to temporarily where they could gather to await transport out of the heavily bombed areas. As one report from Mass Observation noted: "Nobody foresaw the tidal wave of refugees spread all over the country after the first hideous week-end."[41] They were sent to the schools, those large imposing, frequently red-brick buildings, built in the late nineteenth century, under the impetus of W. E. Forster's 1870 Education Act, designed to provide a universal education for all in Britain. Now they were to act as temporary centres where people could rest, be fed and looked after and be found a place to stay for a longer term. That was the theory, but the system simply couldn't cope. Even when Herbert Morrison became Home Secretary in October, the attitude was obtuse, as indicated by a memo in his name covering the period from September to October. "London people lost much sleep and suffered anxiety and discomfort, but there was no breakdown, no panic and no mass evacuation, except in the small heavily bombed areas. The effect was one very largely of surprise. After a few days the first horror of the raids wore off and people became adjusted to the new conditions of shelter life."[42] That was clearly a statement for public consumption and encouragement with little relation to the facts of the matter.

Even as it stumbled in its handling of homelessness, the government strived to reassure its citizens that an attack against one of them was an attack against all. On September 9, the day after Churchill toured the East End, the King and Queen did the same.

According to Reginald William Bell, a leading civil defence officer in the East End, the royal couple was cheered on the occasion "not with hesitation or doubt but with cheers of loyalty."[43] It was said, however, that in some areas they were booed, but exactly why is not quite clear. The Queen famously remarked, after Buckingham Palace was bombed on September 13, that now she could look the East End in the face. Bell rather exaggerates the concern those in the East End felt about the bombing of the Palace.

> There was rage as well as fortitude in the hearts of the people, rage which perhaps reached its height at the time of the day attacks on Buckingham Palace. It was not the bombing of military objectives that aroused their anger, nor even the reasonable "overspill" into residential property around them, but the indiscriminate destruction of their homes. During one afternoon raid, a hefty matron, with arms akimbo, scowled at the sky. "You filthy bastard!" she roared. "*I'd* give you bleedin' *cups of tea*!"[44]

This woman's defiant curse to the sky exemplifies how so many ordinary British citizens were determined not to give in during this new phase of the war. If the German strategy was to try to terrorize them into submission, they were going to remain defiant and carry on. In fact, there was almost a sense that the feared invasion should take place so that the British could demonstrate their ability to deal with the Germans. One letter writer asserted on Tuesday, September 10, "We are all rolling up our sleeves for an invasion and we hope for *this weekend*, at last!"[45] The Reverend John McKenzie almost made it sound like a weekend party in a letter he wrote on September 13 to his niece, the well-known actress Flora Robson, who was then in New York: "The invasion is supposed to be starting today. They have got a lovely day for it, but that is all they will find lovely about it."[46]

For some, it was almost a matter of principle to stay, of not letting the side down. And frequently staying also meant taking a position to help in the war effort: the novelist Elizabeth Bowen was an air raid warden. Possibly her best-known novel is her wartime story *The Heat of the Day* (1949). It takes place in 1942 when the Blitz, in her view, had given the city a fantastic quality. But it hearkens back to the first days of the Blitz, about which she writes evocatively. It was then that Stella met her lover, Robert, who somewhat improbably turns out to be a German spy:

> ... the heady autumn of the first London air raids. Never had any season been more felt; one bought the poetic sense of it with the sense of death. Out of mists of morning charred by the smoke from ruins each day rose to a height of unmisty glitter; between the last of sunset and the first note of the siren the darkening glassy tenseness of evening was drawn fine. From the moment of waking you tasted the sweet autumn not less because of an acridity on the tongue and nostrils; and as the singed dust settled and smoke diluted you felt more and more called upon to observe the daytime as a pure and curious holiday from fear. ... The very soil of the city at this time seemed to generate more strength.[47]

Bowen presented a similar picture, with a greater emphasis on the quiet and emptiness after a raid, in an essay called "England, 1940": "Early September morning in Oxford Street. The smell of charred dust hangs on what should be crystal pure air. Sun, just up, floods the once more innocent sky, strikes silver balloons and the intact building-tops. The whole length of Oxford Street, west to east, is empty, looks polished like a ballroom, glitters with smashed glass." [48]

In Bowen's most famous short story of the war, "Mysterious Kôr," there is an interplay between London and Kôr, the empty African imperial city of H. Rider Haggard's *She*, published in 1887. Bowen had read the novel when she was 12, a few years before the First World War. In 1947, she gave a radio talk about it, quoting the English explorer's description of the city in the novel. "'There, all bathed in the red glow of the setting sun, were miles upon miles of ruins – columns, temples, shrines and palaces of kings.'" As Bowen says, "I saw Kôr before I saw London. ... The idea that life in any capital city must be ephemeral, and with a doom ahead, remained with me – a curious obsession for an Edwardian child." [49] In the short story, Pepita tells her boyfriend Arthur about Kôr as a contrast to noisy blitzed London, but also as if London had become this mysterious silent city. As the story ends:

> With him she looked this way, that way, down the wide, void, pure streets, between statues, pillars and shadows, through archways and colonnades. With him she went up the stairs down which nothing but moon came; with him trod the ermine dust of the endless halls, stood on terraces, mounted the extreme tower, looked down on the statued squares, the wide, void, pure streets. He was the password, but not the answer: it was to Kôr's finality that she turned.[50]

The novelist Margaret Kennedy was in the country while her husband, an eminent judge, remained in London and was serving as an air raid warden. She worried about not hearing from him, but felt that she shouldn't jam up the telephone lines. London was a battle zone. "If he was a soldier I couldn't ring him up in the middle of a battle to ask how he is getting along. I must wait, like a soldier's wife." When she did hear from him, his description of London had a feeling similar to that suggested by Bowen in "Mysterious Kôr."

> David says there is real beauty about London in the blitz. He says it thrills him when he goes on patrol, the blackout makes the houses look much grander, like precipices standing up in the moonlight, and the geometry of the searchlights in the sky. And the A.A. barrage is like a huge orchestra, bursting out into a deafening roar and dying down to a distant grumble. And little pygmy wardens in tin hats run about in the foreground like ants. It sounds the way the *Götterdämmerung* ought to look (and never does) on the stage.[51]

This same sense of grand desolation can be found in Bill Brandt's shadow-filled photographs of London's buildings silhouetted by moonlight in the blackout.

Nevertheless, even as British characteristics of resolve and carrying on came into play, panic was far closer to taking over during this first week of the heaviest bombing raid so far than any were willing to admit later. The sudden appearance of the bombers made Ted Harrison think "Blimey, we've lost the war." Frank Thorpe remarked: "People were really panicking." In one station, an air raid warden remembered, perhaps evoking the Spanish Armada, "Suddenly an armada of bombers came over. We were all looking up at them, saying 'They're ours'. At that moment we had not experienced any bombing at all. Suddenly they let fly. . . . We were completely buried."[52] The Home Intelligence Report for September 9 calmly stated: "The population is showing visible signs of its nerve cracking from constant ordeals." The government was concerned that disorder and chaos, maybe even riots, might erupt, and, in October, it stationed a battalion of the Grenadier Guards in nearby Wanstead in order to be used in the East End. But it was never necessary.[53]

On September 11, Churchill gave a radio address, the first he delivered from the underground War Cabinet rooms close to his official 10 Downing Street residence. In it he did not hide that invasion might well be imminent and that the Germans were busy making preparations for it.

> If this invasion is going to be tried at all, it does not seem that it can be long delayed. ... Therefore, we must regard the next week or so as a very important period in our history. It ranks with the days when the Spanish Armada was approaching the Channel ... or when Nelson stood between us and Napoleon's grand army at Boulogne. ... What is happening now is on a far greater scale and of far more consequence to the life and future of the world and its civilization than these brave old days of the past. ... These cruel, wanton, indiscriminate bombings of London are, of course, a part of Hitler's invasion plans. He hopes, by killing large numbers of civilians, and women and children, that he will terrorize and cow the people of this mighty imperial city, and make them a burden and anxiety to the Government and thus distract our attention unduly from the ferocious onslaught he is preparing. Little does he know the spirit of the British nation, or the tough fibre of the Londoners, whose forebears played a leading part in the establishment of Parliamentary institutions and who have been bred to value freedom far above their lives. This wicked man, the repository and embodiment of many forms

> of soul-destroying hatred, this monstrous product of former wrongs and shame, has now resolved to try to break our famous Island race by a process of indiscriminate slaughter and destruction. What he has done is to kindle a fire in British hearts. . . . He has lighted a fire which will burn with a steady and consuming flame until the last vestiges of Nazi tyranny have been burnt out of Europe.[54]

This address stirred Londoners' resolve to resist Hitler, and helped keep panic at bay. It drew people closer together. It also inspired many in the United States.

VII

The People's War

"It's our nerve versus his"

DURING the summer of 1940, the Germans were aware that through the Battle of Britain they had not achieved air superiority over their one remaining foe. In a memorandum the German Naval Staff wrote: "We have not yet attained the operational conditions which the Naval staff stipulated to the Supreme Command as being essential for the enterprise, namely undisputed air supremacy in the Channel area and the elimination of the enemy's air activity in the assembly area of the German naval forces and ancillary shipping." In terms of Operation Sea Lion, the proposed invasion of the British Isles, the Naval Staff recommended that the Luftwaffe concentrate "less on London and more on Portsmouth and Dover, as well as the naval ports in and near the operational area."[1] Nevertheless, as we have seen, Hitler had been so furious about the bombing of Berlin that he gave in to Goering's wish to concentrate on the bombing of London.

Although that decision ultimately played a crucial role in the Germans losing the war, in the first days of the Blitz the outcome was far from clear. On September 11, 1940, Alan Brooke, the Home Forces commander, noted: "Evidence of impending invasion has been accumulating all day, more ships moving west down the

Channel, intercepted cipher messages, etc." Two days later, he reported, "Spent morning in the office studying increasing evidence of impending invasion. ... Everything looks like an invasion starting tomorrow from the Thames to Plymouth!"[2]

Certainly many Britons were rattled by the first few nights of the Blitz. Some ascribed the use of terror at the time to German national character. For instance, Diana Brinton Lee, who lived in West London near Wormwood Scrubs, wrote, "The idea of general terror ... is in accordance with Hitler's general theories and appeals to the German mind."[3] While Hitler had not specifically ordered the terror bombing of London, there can be no doubt that he realized that, in effect, that was what it was. The raid of September 7 was officially targeted on the huge docks and warehouses along the Thames. If Hitler had wanted to terrorize the more powerful among the population, he could have concentrated on bombing the affluent in the West End. Indeed that might have been more effective in trying to convince, although probably unsuccessfully, those "who counted" that there should be a negotiated peace. Bombing was inaccurate but not to such a degree that it would miss the widespread acreage of the docks and warehouses. As they were located next to the houses of those who worked in them, as well as many others of the poor in the East End, it was inevitable that numerous dwellings would be destroyed and possibly many killed. (Ultimately in the course of the war 40 per cent of London's housing stock was made uninhabitable.)

An editorial in *The Spectator* on September 13 also implied that inducing terror was something Germanic. It analysed the enemy's strategy as a series of failures (although the strategy wasn't quite as unsuccessful as *The Spectator* wished to make it appear) and added, "Now new tactics are invoked. Stark frightfulness, the traditional German *Schrecklichkeit*, is to achieve what relatively legitimate air warfare could not. London is to be desolated, its civilian population slaughtered, ordered life made impossible, by a series of promiscuous attacks that no longer even claim to be directed at military objectives."[4]

This long editorial calmly put forward the possibility of a Nazi landing and attack.

> This is the week in which certain natural conditions – a moon approaching the full, a calm sea and high tides about dawn – favour an attempt at invasion. ... In such a scheme the intimidation of London would play a natural part, in the double hope that disorganisation might be created at the vital centre and forces be detached to defend the capital that should properly be employed to repel aggression. Invasion may or may not be attempted – a very few days will answer that question one way or another.

The Spectator also analysed the strengths and weaknesses of British defences so far. It observed that there was "no effective protection against night bombing." However, anti-aircraft fire was helping. The flotilla of 450 barrage balloons that was stationed over the city soon after September 7 had less military advantage than supposed. They were designed to prevent dive bombing, on the presumption that the bombers might become caught up on the balloons' wires, or that, in order to avoid doing so, the Germans might be compelled to fly so high that it would be difficult for them to pick out their targets. In fact, Nazi bombers did not dive-bomb as a rule, but the presence of the balloons was probably good for the morale of Londoners.

The article ended on a morale-boosting note:

> An enemy bent on only destruction will continue to achieve

> destruction. . . . The savagery is matched, and defeated, by the heroism it evokes, the heroism of the common men and women who know from the first moment the sirens sound at night that they are potential victims, and the active and amazing heroism of the public servants, paid and volunteers, who are coping night after sleepless night with fire and demolition, injury and death, as fire-fighters, wardens, shelter-wardens, St. John and Red Cross staffs and all the rest.[5]

This picture was overly optimistic.

By Sunday, September 15, Alan Brooke, the Commander of the Home Forces, felt that Hitler

> cannot retrace his steps and stop the invasion. The suspense of waiting is very trying especially when one is familiar with the weakness of our defence! ... The responsibility such as that of the defence of this country under the existing conditions is one that weighs on one like a ton of bricks, and it is hard at times to retain the hopeful, confident exterior which is so essential to retain the confidence of those under one, and to guard against their having any doubts as regards final success.

On that day the British bombed, as an anti-invasion move, ports on the continent: Antwerp, Ostend, Calais, and Dunkirk, sinking many German barges in the process. On the 16th, Brooke wrote: "Still no invasion! Rumour has it that tonight is to be the night." But in fact the Germans had concluded that they were losing too many planes, particularly in daylight raids. On that day they lost 165 planes. The final German daylight raid was on September 30, when the Germans lost 47 planes and the British 20.[6]

Eric Sevareid, the American reporter, noted the tipping of the balance:

> [The Germans] did not know that on that day which broke their courage, the back of the Royal Air Force was also broken and that hardly a complete squadron remained in reserve in all the British Isles. Had they been able to continue mass raiding a few more days, it is quite possible that they would have torn an irreparable breach in the barricade of the sky which would have laid England open for successful invasion, altering, perhaps fatally, the outcome of the war. But the Germans lost their nerve; the British did not, and so they won out.[7]

Not until October 3 did Brooke think that the invasion might not take place.[8] And, as late as February 1941, 53 per cent of the population expected that a German invasion would still happen.[9]

In fact, by the middle of September, Hitler was beginning to conclude that his attacks on Britain's air defences were not sufficiently effective, and he delayed Operation Sea Lion, which had been scheduled for late in the month. On October 12, he officially postponed it until the spring of 1941. He persisted in continuing the Blitz until May. However, the nine months of German attacks failed to realize the original definition of Blitz: a quick knockout blow.

In military terms there are two contrary but not necessarily irreconcilable interpretations and consequences of Hitler's decision to bomb London. The first argues that Hitler made a serious tactical error. He might well have been on the verge of winning the Battle of Britain, destroying the British fighter planes and establishing air superiority over Britain. Churchill estimated that from August 24 to September 6 – the period of the most intense

German attack on British air bases – 103 pilots had been killed and 128 severely wounded, and 466 Spitfires and Hurricane fighters had been destroyed or badly damaged. The Germans themselves felt that Britain's fighter defence was definitely weakening.[10] Even if Hitler had not established air superiority over Britain, he was very close, as Sevareid and other commentators had observed.

Yet ultimately the decision to give in to Goering proved to be a cardinal mistake on Hitler's part. As Churchill said at the time: "Never fear, the German soldiers are good, and so are their commanders, but we have one grand friend over there, Corporal Hitler; he'll help us, you mark my words."[11] As Air Vice Marshal Keith Park remarked on September 8, "It was burning all down the river. It was a horrid sight. But I looked down and said: 'Thank God for that', because I knew that the Nazis had switched their attack from the fighter stations thinking they were knocked out. They weren't, but they were pretty groggy."[12] Hugh Dowding, the Air Chief Marshal in charge of Fighter Command during the Battle of Britain, was also relieved that the Germans had stopped bombing RAF airfields. He later commented, "I could hardly believe the Germans would have made such a mistake. From then on it was gradually borne upon me that it was a supernatural intervention at that particular time, and that that [September 7] was really the crucial day."[13] His colleague Park knew the military prognosis had changed; but he "felt confident that we could win as long as I could continue to operate the fighter squadrons."[14] If the Germans had continued their previous line of attack, the air defence of London might have been eliminated completely. As it was, the RAF had time to recuperate, so that by mid-September the British pilots were increasingly successful in downing German planes. (September 15 subsequently became Battle of Britain Day, when the British felt they had won the air battle – even as the Blitz, the bombing battle, went on.)

Although the Blitz ultimately failed, the second interpretation argues that there was a German military justification for the bombing of London. In order to defend London, the British might put at risk as many fighters as they could. The Germans hoped that they would be destroyed by the numerous German fighters that accompanied their bombers. Bombing could also destroy morale and create popular pressure so that the British would sue for peace. This was the objective of terror bombing both at the time of the Blitz and later in the bombing of Germany. Indeed, in my view, the collapse of morale was a real possibility that first weekend in September 1940. But quite rapidly – although bombing continued and the Blitz was destructive of health and strength once sirens, bomb blasts, and anti-aircraft guns made a night's sleep impossible – most Londoners demonstrated their ability to get used to virtually anything. Perhaps the endless bombing and the lack of sleep could have led to the collapse of morale. But neither at the beginning nor during the Blitz did it happen to any significant extent. Quite a few of those who were more prone to panic had left. By the end of the war it was estimated that 2 million Londoners out of the 9 million residents of Greater London had gone, some to stay with family elsewhere, some to reside in country hotels, others trekking eastwards.[15] But the vast majority had no choice but to stay where they were.

Horrible as the Blitz was, ironically it was not ultimately as horrible as expected. That indeed may well have been one factor that made it easier to cope with. As bombs were falling, buildings burning, people dying, the English fit into their role: "It's really not so bad, might be worse, have a cup of tea. I'll put the kettle on." Joanna Mack and Steve Humphries have commented on the role of tea in their 1985 study of *London at War*.

> When all seemed lost there was always the cup of tea. People were observed going back to their homes to find the windows blown in and splinters of glass everywhere, and proceeding calmly to put the kettle on for their morning "cuppa." The propaganda films of the blitz regularly played on this routine to illustrate people carrying on as normal. Tea acquired almost a magical importance in London life. And the reassuring cup of tea actually did seem to help cheer people up in a crisis.[16]

I once met an Englishwoman, a veteran of the Blitz, who immediately told me how grateful she was to the Americans for sending tea!

This attitude of assumed calm and the importance of tea was immortalized in 1960 in a famous sketch, "Aftermyth of War," in *Beyond the Fringe*, the comic review by Alan Bennett, Peter Cooke, Dudley Moore and Jonathan Miller. In it a typical Londoner remarks, "I was out in the garden at the time planting out some deadly nightshade for the Boche. My wife came out to me in the garden and told me the abominable news. 'Thousands have died in Pithy Street,' she said. 'Never you mind the thousands dead,' I said to her, 'you put the kettle on and we'll have a nice cup of tea.'"[17]

The American journalist Vincent Sheean wrote about how the English coped at the time of the Blitz. In the preceding decade, he had noted, in reporting from war-torn Spain and China, how in both countries civilians stoically endured horrible conditions.

> But the English way of resisting terrible adversity is peculiar to the national character. It is neither more nor less courageous than that of other peoples; it is merely different. The difference consists chiefly in the most celebrated of insular mannerisms,

> that which understates and under values. Psychologically this is no doubt a compensatory device of all times, but under the conditions of September and October, 1940, it became almost a mania. A man who had seen his house destroyed and his family's life endangered would have thought himself a sorry knave if he referred to it as anything but "a bit of trouble." The most desperate attack or alarm was referred to as "a flap"; the gravest incident was not thought to justify any undue departure from customary behavior.[18]

This almost conscious cultivation of the phlegmatic attitude can be seen in another example: a cartoon of a housewife cleaning up her house after an air raid. The caption read: "Well, there's one thing about the Blitz, it keeps you busy and you forget about the war."[19] Eric Sevareid also rejected the idea that the British were more heroic than others.

> The people of Britain were brave and heroic in their endurance through those frightful weeks – and so they were. But it would be to make them more than human and thus to do them less than justice to suggest that none at any time betrayed stark fear or that there were no individual cases of panic and hysteria. . . . The British may not be a hot-blooded or excitable people, but they are still people. . . . The day the Germans raided the docks, the first great daylight raid on London . . . I saw terror in the eyes of hundreds as they moved in a great migration away from the awesome pillars of black oil smoke, trudging through snowpiles of powdered glass, pushing their prams, heads turned over shoulders, staring eyes fixed upon the quiet and mocking sky.[20]

England was (and is) a country marked more than most by class differentials. The upper and middle classes affected an insouciance, a casualness, and a stiff upper lip. The prototypical response to the Blitz might be, "Oh, was that a bomb?" The working classes cultivated apathy and cunning as a way of coping with disaster. They could also let themselves go, at least verbally, swearing at Hitler. They were also suspicious of authority, and might well be slow to accept those, frequently from the middle class, who were organizing services to deal with the Blitz.

The bombing was likely to produce two rather contrasting reactions in the civilian population. On the one hand, there was high indignation – how dare the Germans do this to us! Combined with this was a desire to revenge. When Churchill visited the bombed areas there was call for vengeance and retaliatory bombing of Germany. The other possible reaction was panic. John Langdon-Davies, who had observed the bombing in the Spanish Civil War in Barcelona, put forward in *Nerves versus Nazis* (1940) that the Germans would attempt to create panic in their bombing through nervous exhaustion and noise. He argued that the necessity would be simply to get used to it, and that was more or less what happened.[21] Defeatism and a desire for a negotiated peace might have been, in fact, more likely among the middle and upper classes, who had more to lose in the bombing of their homes. The working class tended to be stoical about the war and did their best to continue ordinary life. Surviving the raid at night and going off to their jobs by day was their way of "doing their bit."

Some felt that working-class women might be more prone to panic than working-class men. Both groups were strong-minded and accustomed to hardship and, though grousing, tending to accept what came their way. For the working class in London, it would appear that, unlike many more members of the middle and upper classes, they didn't really believe that there was a serious possibility of invasion, wrong as they were. Despite the evidence of Hitler's extraordinary successes on the Continent, the East Enders simply assumed, against the evidence and not because they were necessarily extremely patriotic, that as before, most recently at the time of the First World War and as long ago as the wars against Napoleon, Britain would win. One Mass Observation diarist observed that although among some Londoners the sirens could induce a sense of panic, in the East End the "vast majority of the people in the areas studied are taking the raids with that curious stolidity that baffles both the enemy and the home propagandist."[22]

That is not to say, of course, that fear and panic did not enter into the popular response. Now that the bombing actually was happening on an unprecedented scale, the weaknesses of the official planning, based on the premise that the raids would be brief and hence shelters need not be designed for long-term occupancy, were plainly evident. In the badly built larger public shelters, there was not enough room on the benches and many had to sit on newspapers on the concrete floors. Animals weren't allowed in public shelters, angering many, and there were no toilet facilities. Especially during the first week of the Blitz, when there were so few anti-aircraft guns in London, there was a depressed feeling that virtually nothing was being done in retaliation; London was defenceless. It was at that moment that some, huddled in crowded fetid shelters, may have felt that there should be a negotiated peace. Barbara Nixon wrote in her memoir *Raiders Overhead* what quite a few felt at the time: "For Londoners there was only a nightmare feeling of impotence; the throbbing Nazi planes could drop their bombs when and where they liked, nobody was doing anything to stop them, and one could only wait for annihilation."[23] In fact, the possibility that a feared spirit of defeatism could be communicated from person to person was one reason the government opposed people sheltering in the tube stations.

While many attempted to hide their fears, there were those who could not or would not. And of course there were terrified and screaming children. The heroic version given in the contemporary press and in such books as Reginald William Bell's *The Bull's Eye* (1943) about the first days of the Blitz was an exaggeration. Bell very much presented the establishment point of view, as a leading civil defence officer in the East End. His account contains a wonderfully backhanded and irritating compliment about those who were not "English," frequently meaning Jews (even though most of those in the East End were English citizens). "What of the fears for the volatile aliens in parts of the East End? There was no panic. There was a good deal of voluntary self-dispersal from some parts, but the staunchness in adversity far surpassed what even experienced observers had expected. The panic-stricken crowds which some had visualised never formed."[24]

The Home Intelligence Reports, then being prepared daily for the Ministry of Information, acknowledged on September 9 the growth of anti-Semitism:

> Owing to the behaviour of the Jews, particularly in the East End, where they are said to show too great a keenness to save their own skins and too little consideration for other people, there are signs of anti-semitic trouble. It is believed locally that this situation may at any moment become extremely serious. This is put forward as an additional reason for a planned dispersal of East End families to be carried out with all speed.

Rather alarmingly, the bad behaviour of Jews is almost taken to be objectively true, with some distancing implied by the use of "said." But at least anti-Semitism is seen as a problem that needs to be dealt with in order to lessen its probable increase.[25]

The daily report on London on September 10 states,

> Exodus from East End growing rapidly. … Increased tension everywhere and when siren goes people run madly for shelter with white faces. Contact spending time in West Ham reports loyalty and confidence in ultimate issue unquenched but nerves worn down to fine point. Conditions of living now almost impossible. … Grumbling and dissatisfaction openly voiced, states Deptford contact. … Class feeling growing because of worse destruction in working class areas; anti-Semitism growing in districts where large proportion of Jews reside owing to their taking places in public shelters early in the day. People in target areas living in shelters; women emerging for short time to do shopping and bolting back again. … Districts less regularly bombed, such as Chelsea and Lewisham, report great neighbourly feeling. Bermondsey Citizens' Advice Bureau inundated with mothers and young children, hysterical and asking to be removed from district.

During the first month of the Blitz, the Home Intelligence Reports often included a section called "Daily Report on Morale," which came on a separate page. For Tuesday, September 10, it claimed, "Morale remains unchanged today," presumably meaning that it is in good shape. This is hard to believe. It does seem a bit desperate and is based on the impression that people are not being defeatist, although they certainly sound close. The report comments on the efforts to get out of London, almost anywhere, by so many people. "There is, however, little evidence that these efforts to escape are due to defeatist feelings, but are simply because the people are thoroughly frightened." The report reaches for psychological straws to help. "Now that they are beginning to feel, are being referred to, as 'soldiers in the front line', everything should be done to encourage this opinion of themselves."

The report suggests that the dead be buried with a Union Jack on their coffins, to indicate that, like members of the military, they died for their country. As far as I know, nothing came of this idea. The report also recommended that postcards be distributed, presumably prepaid, like those issued to the military, so that the poor could send them to relatives outside of London assuring them that they were all right. This would also save on the use of telephone and telegraph. I don't believe anything came of this suggestion either. There is a slight sense of desperation about these comparatively small gestures that would hardly have much effect in alleviating the terrible destruction that was taking place. The need for more mobile canteens is also mentioned and that the voluntary societies involved in providing those and similar services are not able to cope. There is no thought, apparently, at this point that the government should step in. The report's concluding remark perhaps reflects more hope than actuality: "confidence is everywhere expressed in the ability of the metropolitan population to stand up to what they are going through."

The report of the next day, September 11, is somewhat resigned. "Morale is rather more strained than the newspapers suggest. … Factors which contribute to the strain on morale are, of course, as much psychological as material." This time, the only possible action mentioned is the greater use of earplugs! There is also an allusion to the increase of rumours, but no indication of what they are.

(A previous report had the story that Fifth Columnists were using searchlights to help the German bombers.) This report does contain a reasonable explanation for the increase of anti-Semitism.

> This is not so much on account of a marked difference in conduct between Jews and Cockneys, but because the latter, seeking a scapegoat as an outlet for emotional disturbances, pick on the traditional and nearest one. Though many Jewish people regularly congregate and sleep in the public shelters, so also do many of the Gentiles, nor is there any evidence to show that one or the other predominate among those who have evacuated themselves voluntarily through fear or hysteria.[26]

The government did not permit the publication of photographs of the dead. The location of destroyed buildings was not given in the photographs, and particular buildings might be blanked out so exact locations couldn't be determined. News reports did not provide specific locations for buildings destroyed and tended to describe them generically – a school in the East End, or a London hospital, for example. The Ministry of Information stipulated that any photograph or film of bombed buildings had to include a building that had survived. One aim of all this was to limit the information the Germans might acquire, but also to maintain home front morale.[27] Those on the streets knew the reality, even if the dead were removed as quickly as possible. East End schools, though far better built than the slums that had been destroyed, were as vulnerable to bombs as any other structures there – as the tragic case of the South Hallsville School proved.

For those living outside the East End, especially in districts that had not been so hard-hit, it was difficult not to fall into an overly optimistic interpretation of events and to see in the survival of ordinary life the appropriate defiance of the Germans. There are the famous characteristic photographs, a shop with broken windows and a sign, "more open than usual," and the milkman and the postman picking their way through mounds of rubble doing their ordinary deliveries.

There were also those who took advantage of the destruction and confusion during the Blitz. People who left their homes for the shelters later might find that their possessions, such as they were, had been looted. Frank Ball was working in Woolwich Arsenal, and his home was damaged the first weekend and his parents injured.

> While my parents were in hospital and I spent a few days with my sister, the bungalow became a prey to looters, who stripped it bare, not only of damaged goods but anything they could lay their hands on. They even disconnected and stole the kitchen sink. Pilfering was one of the most odious outcomes of the bombings.[28]

When Gladys Streilitz returned home from Maidenhead, where her family had fled on the morning of September 8, she discovered that her home had been looted. "All around us was shattered. We had just had our windows blown out, but people had been in and looted my home and all the bed linen and everything was stolen and, well, we were full of despair."[29] Frank Whipple, a reserve policeman, also noted that there was a great deal of looting: "You'd find bent wardens, heavy rescue men, even police doing it. People were like vultures, going into bombed-out houses and shops and they'd even take rings and valuables off dead bodies."[30]

Looting presented a hard-to-resist temptation, particularly to air raid wardens and firemen who would have had authorized access to empty and bombed premises. Of the reported cases, 42 per cent were committed by such individuals, and 90 per cent of those tried in court had no previous criminal record. It was the impression of Richard L. Jackson of the Criminal Investigation Department that there was no organized looting by gangs, but rather it was done by individuals, seizing the opportunity.[31] In September 1940, 539 cases of looting came to the courts in London, and 1,662 the next month. Yet Angus Calder, a leading figure in presenting a well-rounded picture of the Home Front in his pioneering study *The People's War* (1969) and his shorter successor and more pessimistic volume, *The Myth of the Blitz* (1991), points out that despite the emergence of people behaving badly, the dominant aspect of the myth, the ability of the British to endure and ultimately to triumph, survives without too much difficulty. In recent years, a less optimistic view has come to the fore. For example, Stuart Hylton's 2001 book *Their Darkest Hour* has a much greater emphasis on the looters, the criminals, the black marketeers. Families would take food from bombed shops; children would sift through rubble looking for valuables; even policemen and other rescue workers might take goods on the logic that otherwise they would simply be lost.

An important part of the so-called myth of the Blitz is its sense of a unified people. Again, this was obviously not totally true, although there was greater unity in the face of the desperate need to mobilize to fight Hitler than there had been before. The Blitz was important in increasing the popularity of another crucial phrase, the "People's War," also used by Angus Calder as a book title. There was more "unity" among the people, but it was far from total. They had no choice but to be together, both men and women, in the armed services. But that did not mean that they were always on the best of terms with one another. They had a greater sense of being in some ways a "family." But as we all know, members of families, although they have deep-seated and complex connections, do not necessarily get along and indeed that very closeness can sometimes make cooperation more difficult. One is inevitably reminded of George Orwell's famous definition of England as a family, but with the wrong members in control. The experience of the Blitz played a crucial role in determining that it was not only the armed forces who were involved at the heart of the struggle, but civilians as well. The Blitz helped shape the splendid and rather romantic (and perhaps exaggerated) last paragraph of A. J. P. Taylor's *English History 1914–1945*:

> In the Second World war, the British people came of age. This was a people's war. Not only were their needs considered. They themselves wanted to win. Future historians may see the war as a last struggle for the European balance of power or for the maintenance of Empire. This was not how it appeared to those who lived through it. The British people had set out to destroy Hitler and National Socialism – "Victory at all costs". They succeeded. No English soldier who rode with the tanks into liberated Belgium or saw the German murder camps at Dachau or Buchenwald could doubt that the war had been a noble crusade. The British were the only people who went through both world wars from beginning to end. Yet they remained a peaceful and civilized people, tolerant, patient, and generous. Traditional values lost much of their force. Other values took their place. Imperial greatness was on the way out; the welfare state was on the way in. The British empire declined; the condition of the people improved. Few now sang "Land of Hope and Glory." Few even sang "England Arise." England had risen all the same.[32]

Eric Sevareid noted the growth of friendliness among the British people and the comparative decline of what he called their fear of one another.

> As the crisis mounted, as the realization deepened that they were all together now in the same boat, regardless of accent or income, cap or Homburg, some of the restraints were wearing down, and they became less afraid and easier in company. They began to discover one another, to talk together in train compartments and in the shelters. ... And so it was at this point that a new conception of the war began to take root in the minds of the imaginative and articulate: the idea that Hitler's pressure was accomplishing rapidly what the long struggle of organized working-class British people had been approaching only very slowly. Perhaps we confused the wish with the fact, but we caught sight of a new England: men who had so suffered and achieved in common would no longer fear one another's clothes, accents, or manners. ... Men and women who sacrificed their chill and ugly dwellings for the absorption of the enemy's explosives would demand to return to something better than the slums. ... All that men of social conscience and vision had always insisted could be done was now being done. It was being done to make the nation safe; it could – and would, we thought – be done later to make the people happy. For the first time the war seemed to have taken on a positive meaning.[33]

The term "People's War" is more complex than might at first appear. The raid of September 7 made the conception of the People's War come into its own, and become a more accurate description of the situation. It was used to suggest that this war was genuinely one for democracy – not only in terms of fighting a brutal dictatorship, but because of the extraordinarily high level of citizen participation and commitment. Also there was an implied promise, dramatically unfulfilled after the First World War, that this time the "People" would be "rewarded" after victory.

The phrase had been used as early as September 1939, in a memorandum from the Ministry of Information to the Home Office. "The people should be told that this is a civilians' war, or a People's War."[34] About the same time (September 18, 1939) the phrase appeared in *The Times* in both an article and a letter, tracing it back to the Franco-Prussian War.[35] It was used in the left-wing journal *Tribune* in May 1940.[36] Tom Wintringham in his *New Ways of War* (1940) was another who coined the term. (He was drawing on his experience as a commissar in the International Brigade in the Spanish Civil War to help train the Home Guard.) The term was in the air.

The government knew it needed the people's support, as was suggested in a tactless way (seen as suggesting that the "people's" obligation was to fight for its rulers) in the notorious poster, hastily withdrawn that urged: "Your Courage / Your Cheerfulness / Your Resolution / WILL BRING US VICTORY." Ultimately, the British government did organize the human resources to fight the war, and Churchill gave the "roar" that so profoundly helped. But in many ways the "People" came together themselves, to a degree under the pressure of the Blitz, and they "carried on." Of course this was just the segment of the population that was blitzed, but inevitably many more were aware of that experience. There was little choice, other than hysteria or defeatism.

But thinking about the term the "People" nowadays, we are likely to misunderstand what it meant at the time and to assume that it was an ideal of inclusivity. The "People" who were being bombed were mostly in English urban centres (although Belfast, Cardiff, and Glasgow were also attacked) and they had little interest in including all who might make a claim to be British. This was most notable, ironically, in the case of the Jews, some of whom were as badly blitzed as anyone. As we have seen, despite the Nazis there was a rise of anti-Semitism, particularly in London, as many were convinced that Jews pushed themselves into the best places in the shelters. The term "People's War" implies an achieved unanimity that did not exist.[37] But more positively, it did powerfully and accurately suggest that those on the home front were as much at risk as those who were fighting in the armed forces. Indeed in the early years of the war they were frequently more so.

Even if it was not all heroism and stiff upper lip, the people in the so-called People's War acted better than the authorities expected them to. As September 7 made evident, this was a war in which the "people," not only the military, were in the front line. That point was eloquently stated by J. B. Priestley, the well-known novelist and playwright who, in his persona of a bluff no-nonsense Yorkshireman, gave a series of popular Sunday night broadcasts. On September 8 he emphasized that he personally had no wish to be heroic. He contrasted the experience of the First World War, in which he fought, and the Blitz.

> The fact that now we are nearly all at least within reach of danger seems to me one of the better and not one of the worse features of this war. I consider this an improvement on the last war, in which civilians, who developed some most unpleasant characteristics, lived in security while young men were mown down by the million. ... We are much better off

> now. At least we are sharing such danger as there is, and are not leaning back watching all our young men wither away. ... We see now, when the enemy bombers come roaring at us at all hours, and it's our nerve *versus* his; that we're not really civilians any longer but a mixed lot of soldiers – machine-minding soldiers, milkmen and postmen soldiers, housewife and mother soldiers. ... Instead of being obscure and tucked away, we're bang in the middle of the world's stage with all the spotlights focused on us; we're historical personages, and it's possible that distant generations will find inspiration, when their time of trouble comes, in the report in their history books of our conduct at this hour.[38]

London had become the front line and it was virtually the only one at the time.

Coping triumphed, almost in a negative sense, although it was given a positive spin in the famous phrase "London Can Take It." For example, consider the account recorded later by Daphne Deakin, a resident of Silvertown on the north side of the Thames, opposite Woolwich, an area that was very badly hit on the first night. (One of the iconic pictures of the Blitz depicts German Dornier bombers over Silvertown.) She vividly captures the ordinariness of the tragic. Her statement has an extraordinary flat tone of resigned coping with the situation as it was, when death had caught up with friends and neighbours and the narrator might easily have been killed herself if she had made different decisions that day.

> I remember the Blitz. I was living in Silverto[w]n, London. It interrupted our social life to the extent that we daren't go out in the evenings. Being teenagers, of course, we got a little fed up with that so I remember that my friends and

I decided to go to the Woolwich Granada one Saturday afternoon in September. The idea of going in the afternoon was that we would be able to get home before the German planes came.

Whilst we were in the cinema, at about 5 o'clock a notice came up on the screen to say that an air raid was on and advising everyone to leave and to go to the public Air Raid Shelters outside. We stayed for a while until all of a sudden, without any warning, the cinema shook so we thought it was about time we left!

Everywhere outside was chaotic. By then bombs were literally raining down and we went into the shelter. But people are funny. After a while some of them began to get impatient and started leaving in between each bombing and eventually an Air Raid Warden had to come in and advise everybody to stay there until the "All Clear" had been sounded. Apparently a lot of those who had left between raids had been injured or killed whilst they were out on the streets.

When the "All Clear" went we came out of the shelter to catch the train home from Woolwich to Silverto[w]n. We had to trample over rubble, glass and fires everywhere. Apart from that there weren't any trains running so we had to walk although we weren't quite sure of the way. It was bad enough normally but with the chaos that was around us we were really confused. Then we met one of our neighbours who was coming home from work at the Woolwich Arsenal and he guided us through all the rubble and made a number of detours until we finally reached Silverto[w]n.

When we got there we found we couldn't get to our street because houses had been flattened everywhere, including ours. The neighbour who had so kindly guided us through all the rubble was told that that his wife and son had been killed. In fact she had been coming to the pictures with us but had changed her mind at the last moment. The same fate would have happened to us if we had stayed at home.

My brother, Bill, was home on leave from the Army at the time. He and my other brother, Charlie, had reinforced the shelter in our garden with sand during the morning and when the raid had come, my mother and baby sister, Pat, and my two brothers had been able to lie flat in the shelter. If my sister, Olive, and myself and my father had been there, we would have had to sit up in the shelter and caught the blast.

The neighbours on either side of us were killed through the blast. The houses had direct hits but it was the blast that caught the shelters. One end of our shelter was torn off and when we eventually got there my sister and I had a job to find my mother and young sister. We really believed that they were dead. But fortunately my brother, Bill, had taken them to a school for safety. My brother, Charlie, stayed behind to help get people out of their dug-outs. Dad, at the time, was working at the Woolwich Arsenal and so he didn't find us till next day. Believe it it was a relief when we all got together again.

We lived in a church hall until they found us living accommodation and then it was a question of furniture and clothing, because all that was left was what we literally stood up in. We had no furniture or clothing because everything had been destroyed in that one raid whilst we had been at the pictures.[39]

Mass Observation reported a conversation on September 10, 1940, about death. "'It might be anyone. It might be *anyone*. …

It's not fair we should have to suffer like this! We never thought it coming. It's coming to all of us.' 'It has come, lady, it has come. It's here for us all, We're alive now, we might be dead tonight,' said an elderly man."[40]

That night one fire-watcher at St Paul's Cathedral remarked to another: "It's like the end of the world." To which the other replied: "It's the end of *a* world."[41] As Rebecca West remarked: "It could not have been predicted that aerial warfare ... should utterly defeat its users by transforming those who suffer it to the most glorious of individuals. This sly and exalted achievement of history at one stroke regenerated the town-dweller ... and lent him the innocence of the front-line soldier; it gave a promise that life can transcend itself."[42]

The bombing of London did not lead to the defeat of the nation attacked. The Blitz also demonstrated that flawed as human beings are, and imperfect as their responses may be, terror very rarely, ultimately, achieves its objects and human beings have, most fortunately, the power of survival physically, mentally and spiritually.

VIII

An Ideal but Impermanent City

"Whoever gets it next, it won't be you"

WHAT is always quite amazing about such emergency situations as the Blitz is the degree to which ordinary life goes on. That was certainly true of artists, writers and the bohemians and intellectuals who helped make London a cultural as well as political capital. Of course, they were not unaffected by the bombing; their reactions to the events of September 7 and the ensuing months of the Blitz, while more articulate than those of the working class in the East End, are no less valid or worthy of examination.

Two literary journals, Cyril Connolly's *Horizon* and John Lehmann's *New Writing*, had as their purpose the continuation of culture during wartime. Although with the onslaught of the heavier bombing in London many theatres and cinemas closed, publishing continued. Despite the shortage of paper, numerous "ordinary" books still did appear. (Severe paper rationing made books more and more valued. Consider the sad but also triumphant notice in T. C. Worsley's *The End of the "Old School Tie"*, a volume in the Searchlight series: "First printed April, 1941, and destroyed by enemy action. Reset in May and published in June 1941.") The culture one was fighting for had to continue to exist – otherwise, what was the fight for? Myra Hess's noontime concerts at London's National Gallery were a famous example of that. Her most renowned playing was of Beethoven and Bach, making the point that the true international German culture was being fought for in the war against the Nazis.

In the March 1940 issue of *Time and Tide*, George Orwell reviewed *War Begins at Home*, the Mass Observation book on the first four months of the war. Mass Observation had reported that people were bored by the Phoney War, and that they also assumed that Britain would win (an assumption that September 7, 1940 would do surprisingly little to change). The book also made clear that the government was at too far a remove from the people. But Orwell maintained that Mass Observation itself was run by those who did not understand the ordinary person. It exaggerated, he believed, the people's apathy, lack of interest, and misunderstood its "grumbling," which was a way of letting off steam rather than being anything more significant. It did not appreciate, Orwell felt, the patriotism of the people. "The majority of human beings, always and everywhere, are vaguely discontented with their lot, and in countries where free speech is permitted it is the rarest thing in the world to hear a friendly comment on the Government in power at the moment." He nevertheless recognized that there was a problem of morale. "In war it is civilian morale, especially working-class morale, that is decisive in the long run, and there is little or no sign that the Government recognizes this."[1]

Meanwhile, the Ministry of Information was trying to improve morale. Through the use of Home Intelligence Reports and actually employing Mass Observation itself, the authorities attempted to discover what people were thinking. (Rather than being carefully researched, the Intelligence Reports were highly impressionistic documents. Individuals in the Ministry called on regional officials, professional figures such as doctors, and others they might know who they thought would have a sense of what people were thinking. At the end of September 1940, an attempt was made to make the reports more systematic, using such sources as the Mass Observation organization, Police Duty Room reports, and BBC Listener Research.[2] The brief reports, frequently only a page in length, were extremely interesting in what they did say, and their rather feeble suggestions about how to cope. In the best authoritative manner of the British civil service, they had that total tone of assurance that their assessments were accurate.)

Orwell himself became more optimistic within the context of a dire situation. On May 10, 1940, the day Winston Churchill was named Prime Minister, Orwell joined the Home Guard, where his experience in the Spanish Civil War was very useful. Six weeks later, on June 22, he wrote a letter to *Time and Tide* calling for the arming of the people in order to help repel the invasion that he felt would take place "within the next few days or weeks. . . . For the first time in decades we have a Government with imagination, and there is at least a chance that they will listen."[3]

Orwell's wartime diary is rather calm about the September 7 attack. His initial reaction was essentially that the Blitz was a great nuisance. He noted on September 10, "It is not so much that the bombing is worrying in itself as that the disorganisation of traffic, frequent difficulty of telephoning, shutting of shops whenever there is a raid on, etc., etc., combined with the necessity of getting on with one's ordinary work, wear one out and turn life into a constant scramble to catch up lost time." He went on to describe bombing, finding it on the whole less disconcerting than his experiences fighting in the Spanish Civil War. "All over South

London, little groups of disconsolate-looking people wandering about with suitcases and bundles, either people who have been rendered homeless or, in more cases, who have been turned out by the authorities because of an unexploded bomb."

After spending the night in a public shelter, Orwell describes

> people, mostly elderly working class, grousing bitterly about the hardness of the seats and the longness of the night, but no defeatist talk. ... I should think 3 months of continuous raids at the same intensity as the last 4 nights would break down everyone's morale. But it is doubtful whether anyone could keep up the attack on such a scale for 3 months, especially when he is suffering much the same himself.

In both parts of this prediction, Orwell was wrong. He believed that the British retaliatory raids were effective, which was far from true. The heavy raids on London did keep up for another two months, and then for another month at not so severe a level. And, of course, the London Blitz lasted eight months in all, until May 10, 1941. Contrary to what Orwell thought, the continuance of the bombing made it, I believe, easier to bear rather than harder. Horrible as it was, through familiarity and the discovery that one survived, the air attacks diminished in effectiveness.

On September 12, Orwell pointed out the growth of friendliness, a common comment about the effect of the Blitz. But the question of the permanence of this sort of change is suggested in an emblematic story told by the novelist Elizabeth Taylor. At some point after the Blitz was over, a working-class chap started up a conversation with a toff in a train. He cut the conversation off, saying "Do you mind, it isn't the blitz any longer."[4] Those who talked too much about their Blitz experiences became known as

Bomb Bores and an unspoken agreement was reached – if one person told a bomb story, the other person's bomb story had to be listened to as well. Yet, James Burbridge, an engineer in Plumstead in southeast London, commented on his experience on September 7 in the diary he kept for Mass Observation: "Went through most terrifying experience, so far, of this war." He went to a shelter. "There were 8 people here, that is four couples, as it happened, all strangers. As the night wore on, we became quite friendly, communicative & even intimate."[5]

Orwell also recounted his conversation with a young man who believed Hitler would win, that the war was being fought for the rich, and agreed with Orwell that it would end with revolution. Orwell compared the atmosphere in the capital to St Petersburg in 1916. "With all this [the young man] was not unpatriotic." Orwell also mentioned to him Churchill's visit to the East End on that first Blitz Sunday and Churchill's alleged comment that it was "not so bad." "The youth: 'I'd have wrung his bloody neck if he'd said it to me.'" Orwell observed with some exaggeration, "The havoc in the East and South London is terrible, by all accounts." And he bemoaned that his platoon of Home Guards was not sufficiently armed to be very effective against invasion.[6]

The Churchill story – and the "not so bad" comment – seem extremely unlikely. On the contrary, while working in 1946 on his history of the war, Churchill couldn't remember the details of the tour he took that day and so checked with General Ismay, who had accompanied him. Ismay wrote back to him about their viewing a shelter where 40 had died: "It was a most moving scene. You broke down completely and I nearly did. ... I heard an old woman say, 'You see, he really cares, he's crying.'"[7]

Orwell concentrates far more on the personal when he revisits the events of September 7 in his diary the following spring. On

April 8, 1941, he recorded his reading of *The Battle of Britain*, a Ministry of Information publication.

> It is the first official account ... of the first great air battle in history – it is a pity that they did not have the sense to avoid the propagandist note altogether. The pamphlet is full of "heroic", "glorious exploits," etc., and the Germans are spoken of more or less slightingly. Why couldn't they simply give a cold accurate account of the facts, which after all are favourable enough?

Reading it makes him think how undramatic great events might be when you are actually participating in them. Now in April he has a whole different set of "vivid" memories ("mostly of trivial things") than those he recorded the first time around. He now remembers that he was to have tea – that eternal beverage – with Cyril Connolly. On his way, Orwell observed on the bus

> two women in front of me insisting that shell-bursts in the sky were parachutes, till I had a hard job of it not to chip in and correct them. Then sheltering in a doorway in Piccadilly from falling shrapnel, just as one might shelter from a cloudburst. Then a long line of German planes filing across the sky, and some very young R.A.F. and naval officers running out of one of the hotels and passing a pair of field glasses from hand to hand.

He joined Hugh Slater, a writer, and Connolly in the latter's flat on the top floor of Athenaeum Court on Piccadilly, and the three men watched the large fires that had broken out on the other side of St Paul's with "the great plume of smoke from an oil drum somewhere down the river." Slater sat in the window seat and compared the scene nostalgically to Madrid. There was apparently no inclination to seek shelter and indeed Connolly led his guests up to the rooftop, where he regarded the scene below and said, "It's the end of capitalism. It's a judgment upon us." Connolly captured the same feeling in a more ironic way in the title of his book of essays, published in 1945: *The Condemned Playground*. Orwell remarks that he didn't agree with his host's view, "but was chiefly struck by the size and beauty of the flames. That night I was woken up [he was then living near Regent's Park] by the explosions and actually went out into the street to see if the fires were still alight – as a matter of fact it was almost as bright as day, even in the N.W. quarter – but still didn't feel as though any important historical event were happening."[8]

Orwell summed up his impression of the significance of the Blitz, and particularly its first day, in the first "London Letter" he wrote for *Partisan Review*, the New York left-wing intellectual journal. He composed it in January 1941 while the Blitz was still going on:

> The air-raids ... make continuous intellectual life very difficult. I don't mean because of physical danger. It is true that by this time everyone in London has had at least one "providential escape" – these so common that it is now considered bad form to talk about them – but the actual casualties are very few, and even the damage, though enormous, is mostly localised to the City of London and the East End slums. But the disorganisation of transport, communications, etc., causes endless inconvenience. ... When all is said and done one's main impression is the immense stolidity of ordinary people, the widespread vague consciousness that things can never be the same again, and yet, together with that, the tendency of life

> to slip back into the familiar pattern. On the day in September when the Germans broke through and set the docks on fire, I think few people can have watched those enormous fires without feeling that this was the end of an epoch. One seemed to feel that the immense changes through which our society has got to pass were going to happen there and then. But to an astonishing extent things have slipped back to normal.[9]

Julian Symons was nine years younger than George Orwell. Later he would become both better known than Orwell and a good friend of his, but in 1940 he was an obscure writer who edited a poetry journal. He was also then a Trotskyist attempting to be a conscientious objector on the basis that he didn't believe in fighting in a capitalist war (this failed to work, and soon he would be mobilized into the army). His recollection of the beginning of the Blitz also speaks of the contrast between the dramatic and the mundane. He spent the day with the poet Roy Fuller:

> September 7, 1940. Armageddon Day. On this Saturday afternoon Roy Fuller and I went swimming in Brockwell Park. From a hill in the park we watched the tiny birds far overhead in the blue sky, dozens of them moving in formation undisturbed by the coughing tubes that puffed smoke around them. Very soon the crump of bombs sounded from the East End, and more flights of birds swam across the sky. The destruction of London had begun. It was the fulfilment of the prophecies we had been making for years, and there was nothing to be done about it. We went back to the house in Denmark Hill where I was living, and from there just a few steps up the road to a pub called The Fox Under the Hill, where we drank and played bar skittles until closing time.

Symons's attitude reflected that of many on the left who had expended their enthusiasm on behalf of the Republicans in the Spanish Civil War, which was when, they believed, the stand against fascism needed to be taken; now they had limited enthusiasm for their own country. By late 1940 the dominant attitude was one of resignation to the inevitable war. C. Day Lewis had written, "Spain was a death to us, Munich a mourning." In his poem "Where Are the War Poets," responding to a call for heroic verse, and explaining why it wouldn't appear, Day Lewis wrote:

> It is the logic of our times,
> No subject for immortal verse –
> That we who lived by honest dreams
> Defend the bad against the worse.

Ironically, Symons found the atmosphere created by the bombings in London quite wonderful. It was similar to the sense of utopia that Orwell felt in Barcelona in the early months of the Spanish Civil War, recorded in *Homage to Catalonia*.

> A wretched time, people say. I recall it as one of the happiest periods of my life. I have always desired a society in which everything should be impermanent and in which the possession of property and the inheritance of money should be eliminated. It did not disturb me at all to know that the place in which I lived might any day be destroyed, and the routines by which most of us live become meaningless. I know now that I shall never see such a Utopia, but life in London at this time gave a hint of it, as life in Russia must have done in the months after the Revolution. For such a temperament London in those days was in many ways an ideal city. The

> journey to work was an adventure and an absurdity – twice a bomb fell within a hundred yards of the bus in which I was travelling. Living became a matter of the next meal, the next drink. The way in which people behaved to each other relaxed strangely. Barriers of class and circumstance disappeared, so that London was more nearly an equalitarian city than it has ever been in the last quarter of a century. Was it mere romanticism that discovered "new styles of architecture, a change of heart" [a famous line by W. H. Auden] in the bombed places?[10]

The artist Elizabeth Watson responded in a similar way to Symons to the planes in the sky. She served as an ambulance driver in London during the Blitz. "One Saturday afternoon there was the most beautiful raid. ... Five hundred or so Nazi planes flew over London so high that they looked like tiny silver slivers floating silently above. When our fighters arrived they rolled and wheeled like flocks of seagulls skimming over the sea in a gale. How could such a wonderful sight be the herald of death?"[11]

Vera Brittain was also in London on September 7. She was a prominent pacifist, famous for *Testament of Youth*, her account of her experiences during the First World War, when she served as a nurse in France. She was an opponent of bombing by either side, and did not hesitate to express her opinions, even during the war. In 1941 she published *England's Hour: An Autobiography 1939–1941*, intended to be a report on her life in London, as well as a general political account of those years, one that did not neglect her pacifist message. She emphasized the desolation of London, the many who had left, the empty houses in Chelsea and Kensington. She looked out on the Thames in mid-August from her house in Chelsea. "By sitting in my own window for half an hour, I can see as much war preparation as I saw in Étaples village during 1917. In those days, the London newspapers used to remark that the Zeppelin raids 'brought it home to us'. It is coming home to us now in deed and in truth. We in London have not much longer to wait."[12]

She continued to write on pacifist values while also being very active in arranging the evacuation of children overseas. Her son and daughter (the latter grew up to be the well-known politician Shirley Williams) had gone to the United States, where Brittain had been frequently herself with her British husband, George Catlin, who taught at Cornell University. She found the early raids quite serious, but she did realize that with September 7 there was an increase both in seriousness and intensity.

> With all my family overseas, London herself became my companion. Never, it seems to me, has she looked so beautiful as during these hours when she faces an ordeal the like of which she has never known through the centuries of her history. Outside the windows of our lonely house, the Thames from Westminster to Putney coils like a shining serpent basking in sunshine.[13]

Saturday afternoon, the 7th, Brittain attended a conference on Oxford Street, walked in Hyde Park, and having somehow missed the sirens was startled to see German planes above. She took a taxi to the house of a friend in Kensington, where she had been staying after her husband had left for the United States to teach. (A nearby time-bomb had made it unwise for her to remain in her Chelsea house.) Brittain and her friend went to the roof to observe the dockland fires. Then, from the drawing room, they heard church bells and wondered rather casually if the invasion had started. The maid came in and recommended that they peek out the curtain and observe the fires.

> I was just turning to look when a blow such as I have never known even in nightmares seems to strike the house like a gigantic flail. I am swept off my feet and out of my senses; somehow, a second later, I find myself in the basement, but even before I arrive there, a second terrific crash makes the whole earth rock like a ship in mountainous seas. The cook, already below, tells us later that the house appeared to gather itself up and pitch forward. . . . The blast has blown glass from the leaded panes, though the windows were open, sulphur fumes, thick and acrid, pour through the passages. . . . I go to the telephone with the abnormal calm that for most of us follows an escape from death before the reaction begins.

She called the police, suggesting that they take a look at the house after the raid is over. The police appeared immediately and reported that seven bombs were dropped in a quarter-mile area. The damage was quite extensive. "Sitting in the basement when the police have gone holding a cup of tea in hands now ignobly shaking, I reflect that shock is quite bad enough. Wondering whether my face is as green as the faces of the others, I contemplate with astonishment the fact that I am still alive."[14] This comes very close to being contrary to what a taxi driver had told her a few days before. "You always believe . . . that whoever gets it next, it won't be you. That's what enables people to carry on."[15]

Chelsea conformed to its bohemian reputation in the memoirs of Theodora FitzGibbon, who later became a well-known cookbook writer. She was then living with the photographer and painter Peter Rose Pulham. Her life is wonderfully summarized in Paul Levy's entry about her in the *Oxford Dictionary of National Biography.*

> In Paris for a fortnight in 1938, she met the successful photographer (and less successful surrealist painter) Peter Rose Pulham (1910–1956) and began an affair. Through him she met Balthus, Cocteau, Dalí, and Picasso in Paris, and then in London, after a dramatic escape from France by bicycle and boat from Bordeaux, she worked for a time for the Free French, befriended the poet Brian Howard, stayed at Rosa Lewis's Cavendish Hotel, and consorted with both the frogman Commander Crabbe and the Soviet spy Donald Maclean. At the one-room Colony Club, the Horseshoe, and the Mandrake, she and Pulham drank with the young painters John Banting, John Minton, Lucian Freud, and Francis Bacon. The affair with Pulham ended in 1943, after Theodora had met the Irish-American writer (Robert Louis) Constantine Lee-Dillon FitzGibbon (1919–1983). ... FitzGibbon and Theodora were married, at Chelsea register office on 21 March 1944. Dylan Thomas was to have been one of the witnesses, but arrived too late for the ceremony: he wrote a version of "At last, in a wrong rain" for their wedding anniversary. The marriage lasted fifteen years, and was often stormy. It ended in divorce in 1959, when Theodora found FitzGibbon in bed with one of her house guests. The following day they complimented her on the *bœuf à la mode* she had left in the kitchen.

Indeed, it would be on September 7, 1940 that Theodora met Dylan Thomas, and their day was appropriately boozy. They ignored the first siren, drinking the wine on hand, and then about five decided to go out to a pub along with Pulham and other friends. The King's Head and Eight Bells was unusually crowded as people were afraid (although not sufficiently frightened to go to shelters) and had come there in search of news and companionship.

> At about six-thirty the "all clear" sounded, and by then the sky was the colour of a blood orange, a seething flaming mass. … After a year of the blackout it was weird to have light again, but it was an ominous brightness. … Inside the pub, everybody was speculating as to what had happened on this sunny, Saturday, September afternoon. Jokes were made to relieve the tension; beer mugs were put down more noisily to shut down other sounds. We were glued together by dread. All our eyes were rounder, the pupils enlarged, and although we laughed, our lips twitched with alarm. … We did not know it then, but the winter of the bombs, or the Blitz as it was called, had begun.

She continues with the next day, September 8, and the difficulties of life in the targeted city.

> There was no gas to cook the breakfast with, so in a combined operation we made toast and coffee over an electric fire lying on its back, and cooked kippers on the flat part of an electric iron … Dylan has spent what was left of the night on the sitting-room sofa. The government communiqué on the wireless said: "Fires were caused among industrial targets. Damage was done to lighting, and other public services, and some dislocation to communications was caused. Attacks have also been directed against the docks. Information as to

> casualties is not yet available". "That," said Dylan, "is the understatement of all time."[16]

The use of the passive voice in the announcement deprived the Germans of agency and credit. As with the famous phrase, "Fires Were Started," the authorities minimized the effects of the Blitz through language.

Theodora and her friends were a rather friendly and loving group to begin with, but she commented perceptively, "Despite all the horrors, the Blitz was not entirely destructive, for it produced a marked change in the attitude of British people to one another. Experiencing a common danger made for a friendliness, almost love, amongst total strangers." Simone Weil, who was in England during 1943, the last year of her life, made the same point: "What strikes me most about these people, in their present situation, is a good humor that is neither spontaneous nor artificial, but that comes from a feeling of fraternal and tender comradeship in a common ordeal."[17]

Theodora went on in her account:

> Everybody was in love with life and living. … Social and sexual distinctions were swept away and, when a dramatic change such as that takes place, it never goes back in quite the same way. … For the young it was undeniably exciting and stimulating. It was God's gift to naughty girls, for from the moment the sirens went, they were not expected to get home until morning when the 'all clear' sounded. In fact, they were urged to stay where they were. When it came to the pinch, where their parents were concerned, fate was far preferable to death. … Young people were reluctant to contemplate death without having shared their bodies with someone else. It was

> sex at its sweetest: not for money or marriage, but for love of being alive and wanting to give.[18]

As we have seen, the Blitz in fact provided a suitable occasion for some young women to lose their virginity.

Many novels, stories, and poems, were written about the Blitz, but few specifically deal with September 7. In 1942, Molly Lefebure published a short story with a pointed title, "Night in the Front Line," which most likely takes place on September 7, although it is not stated explicitly. The central character, the Cockney Mrs Minnow, is bombed out of her house and is sent to a rest centre at a school. It too is bombed. She has a narrow escape there and then moves on to a deeper shelter. "When the All Clear sounded, she ascended into a desolate, smoking, reeking wasteland which had been her world and was now a dark pile of ruins." She goes to the docks to look for her husband, but is not allowed through. She wishes to go home, but remembering she has no home to go to, she joins the stream of refugees going east, planning to stay with her sister in Chingford. " 'Couldn't bear another night, I couldn't, drive me mad. ... Everythink gone. ... No light. No gas. Nothink but me purse and me pensions book. Nothink. My God, what a blooming awful world it is.' "[19] There is hardly an heroic depiction of the Blitz here – only despair and agony and loss.

Of even more interest in this regard is Lefebure's brilliant but overlooked 1988 novel, *Blitz!* The protagonist, the very young Morweena Duchamp, is a reporter in east London during the war (as was her creator; after the war Lefebure worked for 15 years as a youth counsellor for the Greater London Council and then became a full-time writer, specializing in literary biography). *Blitz!*

begins during the Phoney War and a staged dress rehearsal for a raid that its heroine is covering, and ends in the spring of 1941, when the London Blitz is over. Among the central characters are the gentry Sowersby family. The two sons are in the military (Jos, the elder, is a fighter pilot), and the daughter is in the Women's Voluntary Service, in charge of billeting. There is also an extended Cockney family who sustain terrible losses; they establish residence in a shelter, one that at first is totally chaotic and unstructured until Odile, Morweena's sister, becomes its self-appointed shelter-marshal. Marie, the head of the Cockney family, eventually becomes her second in command. Two nurses also work in the shelter, but they are the total staff for hundreds of people. Buckets are the only sanitation; chemical lavatories are promised but never appear. The Blitz itself, and particularly its first day, dominates the novel.

The middle- and upper-class characters are the more fully developed figures in the novel and are those who act, while the working class is more acted upon. Yet nevertheless the Cockney family is the heart of the book. As in the title of Lefebure's short story, they are on the front line – indeed in a sense practically the only British front line at the time until the fighting started in North Africa. Most of the characters are acting well and working extremely hard for the war effort. It is simply what one does. At the centre of the book is the description of the experience of Marie and her family on September 7. They have just returned from the traditional Cockney paid holiday of hop picking in Kent. Although the genesis of the story lies in Lefebure's 1942 tale, these Cockneys, unlike Mrs Minnow, are determined to stay in the East End of London.

Although other cities had been bombed before, none was as large as London. Civilians of the modern world now realized even more vividly that they were vulnerable, that they were potential victims. A city being bombed meant that anyone in it might be killed or wounded by chance. At the same time, since such a fate had so much arbitrariness, on the whole one had no choice but to conduct one's life as Vera Brittain's taxi driver had advised: as if it couldn't really happen. One could take reasonable precautions, but they lessened one's chances of being out of harm's way only to a degree. Fate and happenstance still determined whether one survived.

Perhaps as a result, people tried to carry on with their daily lives as much as they could. After three weeks of bombing, for instance, Leslie Jerman, the 19-year-old future journalist, slept in his own bed, despite the risk, while eight others in his family in East Ham stayed in the backyard Anderson shelter. "Our windows went. … Sometimes the gas went off. The postman still came every morning." He would also stay at the office – he was working as an office boy in the London office of *The Scotsman* – where a shelter was improvised in the basement. "One night the gas main in Bouverie Street was hit. Our caretaker, Mrs Wright, hung a kettle on an iron rod over it to boil water for tea. … We tended to become accustomed to bombing. The horror stories were a commonplace. Then we got tired of people's dramatic bomb stories and told them: 'I'll listen to yours if you hear mine.'" (Bomb Bores were even more of a problem at work than on trains, it appears.) "There was an extraordinary sense of unity of purpose and strangers talked to each other. This was the loveliest recollection I have of that time."[20]

The editor of *PM*, Ralph Ingersoll, came over from New York to write his *Report on England: November, 1940*, in which he recorded both the heroism that he found in London, as well as the ordinariness. He emphasized the dramatic aspect of what was happening, suggesting that the first days of bombing were the most important. "The battle that was fought in the air over London between September 7 and 15 may go down in history as a battle as important as Waterloo or Gettysburg. Like Gettysburg, it may be recorded as a battle that the loser had won and didn't know it."

And then at the very end of his short book, he summed up the quality of the reaction to the German bombing by quoting a letter from the department store Selfridge's. Throughout the war there was a great emphasis in London on "business as usual." This might seem overly commercial; similarly, some thought the same about the "America Open for Business" posters that appeared in the United States in the wake of the 9/11 attacks. Perhaps in both cases, it was a legitimate response to terror – that ordinary life goes on. Ingersoll said about the Selfridge's letter that it could be called "a masterpiece of British understatement, of faultless commercial calm. Whatever it is, it's one of the few exhibits I have from London about which I can honestly and genuinely and without qualification say the word 'Typical.'" The letter written in September in response to a complaining customer concerns the failure of Selfridge's to supply some groceries:

> Dear Madam,
>
> As you have doubtless read in the Press, on the night of the 18th inst. we were selected by enemy raiders as a "Military Objective," but fortunately the Store only received slight damage and had it not been for the delayed action bombs in the neighbourhood we should have opened as usual the following morning.
>
> The fact that the authorities prevented us from opening caused a certain amount of inconvenience to our customers, which is much regretted. ... If by any chance you were put to any inconvenience, we feel sure you will appreciate that

> the circumstances were entirely beyond our control, but we are happy to inform you that every department in the Store (including the Provision Section) is now functioning quite normally.[21]

Ingersoll's countryman Vincent Sheean noted that many Londoners felt that they were obliged to stay in town to demonstrate that they weren't afraid, to "fly the flag." Others fled and may have had doubts that Britain could win. Sheean, writing before the United States entered the war, agreed it would not be won until the United States and the Soviet Union came in on the side of the Allies. The British government was dedicating itself to wooing the Americans. Churchill was busily establishing his special relationship with Franklin Roosevelt. Through Lend-Lease, the United States was aiding Britain but it was certainly unclear in September 1940 when and if the United States would join in. Since the Nazi–Soviet Pact of August 1939, Russia was practically an enemy. The most Britain could valiantly strive to do was not to lose the war. That, too, made it particularly important that London did not break under this extraordinary onslaught.

As the Blitz continued, psychologists and psychiatrists were quick to study the effect of nightly air raids on British civilians. Early in the war, a series of articles appeared on the effects of the Blitz in the *International Journal of Psycho-Analysis*. It had been expected that the Blitz would cause a high degree of war neurosis and that bombing would be, to some degree, the equivalent of actually being in the trenches. Hence, there would be little difference between the battle front and the home front. In an article, Edward Glover compared it to a long-drawn-out earthquake, but he pointed out that there was not in fact an easy equivalent between the front and the home front.[22]

Civilians are only part-time soldiers. It is true they are exposed to danger, much as a soldier on the front line, but they are deprived of the ability of striking back possessed by military forces. Most of the time the civilian is leading an ordinary life, removed from military discipline, and has the support of family, friends and community. If a civilian had the equivalent of shell shock and was hospitalized, that would not necessarily place him or her, at least in theory, in a safe location, unlike a soldier returned from the front. It would also remove the individuals from their support group. The obligation, except for the air raid wardens and firemen, was to endure, to "take it," rather than to engage in any positive action. And there was even among some a sense of exhilaration. "During the first September raids people of naturally good spirit tended to be excited and elated by the experience of being bombed. They were very communicative about their experiences and escapes and laughed and joked with some excitement about 'still being alive.'"[23]

If panic were to overtake the London population, it would have been most likely during the night of September 7. That didn't happen. Ironically, as Glover observes, this led to overly optimistic conclusions. Before the war broke out, the assumption was that the population, if bombed, would be subject to mass neurosis, would indeed be subject to mass panic, as had been predicted in novels by H. G. Wells and others. In some hospitals, mental wards were evacuated in order to make room for Londoners shell shocked by the raids.[24] When that did not occur, there was then a tendency to move too easily to the opposite scenario: that there was no panic whatsoever, and that the Londoners could "take it" with great ease. This wasn't true either, and there were cases of collapse and inability to cope. But they were far fewer than expected, perhaps because so many who felt particularly threatened actually left London.

The psychoanalyst Melitta Schmideberg commented on reactions to the early days of the London Blitz:

> In the first week of the blitz people in the street looked tired and worn, partly owing to lack of sleep. Some were nicer than usual and made a point of reassuring others, while some were frightened and irritable. ... The raiders arrived with such clockwork regularity every evening that people would merely look up at the sky with the comment "Here they come!" or if they were a few minutes later, "What's the matter, Adolf? Short of planes?" ... An indifference developed which in normal times would have been regarded as callousness. There was only slight exaggeration in a remark made by a friend of mine to the effect that if you heard the most ear-splitting noise and a shock like an earthquake you would merely say: "Oh! That's nothing! It's only the next door house that's gone!"[25]

Schmideberg's conclusion about the effects of the Blitz are quite intriguing:

> There were very much fewer dramatic reactions to the raids than had been expected. It is true that a number of cases of "raid-shock" have probably escaped observation and that many of those who could not stand the raids left for the country. But the majority of the population adapted itself to the new "blitz-reality." It did so by acquiring new standards of safety and danger and by gradually learning to take the bombing as an unpleasant but unavoidable part of life. Fearlessness was usually based on the secret conviction "I cannot be

> hurt" – an emotional denial of the possibility of being hurt and regression to the narcissism of the baby. Adaptation was helped by identification with those less frightened than oneself and "projection" of the frightened part of oneself on to more timid people. Activity, providing a sublimated outlet for aggressiveness and countering the feeling of helplessness, was a help. Rational fears were increased by irrational ones. Yet the "blitz situation" also provided ample libidinal, sadistic and masochistic satisfaction. The condition of certain neurotics improved.[26]

Being bombed night after night for eight to ten hours was traumatic. But it was also a situation that one became accustomed to. Even terror can become habitual, one's ordinary expectation. And there was only so much that one could do about it. There were precautions, reinforcing rooms, going into the cellar or under the stairs or going to shelters, either to an Anderson or a communal one. Irving Janis, in his *Air War and Emotional Stress: Psychological Studies of Bombing and Civilian Defense* (1951), came to some interesting conclusions about the effect of the raids in London and elsewhere. Air raids might well have been a factor in breakdowns yet, in fact, admissions to mental hospitals decreased slightly. He found that the timid frequently became less so because of the experience of the raids: they discovered that they could take it better than they expected. The beginning of a raid, because of the noise, might be very frightening, but then – in many cases in as short a period as a quarter of an hour – people became used to the situation. There was almost a sense of relief that the raids had started, as the period of expectation took its own sort of toll.

Janis writes, "With successive dangerous raids, the bombed population displayed more and more indifference towards air attacks. ... Bombings came to be regarded with a degree of detachment that approached the usual attitude toward peacetime traffic dangers."[27] On the other hand, Anthony Wohl, the eminent historian of modern Britain, who was only three and a half at the time, and living in London, remembers his mother in a state of constant fear. But it did not translate into defeatism. There was a sense of fatality. With extraordinary restraint, in a pamphlet about the fire service published in 1941, the anonymous author introduced Black Saturday as follows: "On 7th September 1940, the gentlemen of blood and iron came flying in their Dorniers and Heinkels to shower their bombs of fire and high explosive over the East End of London."[28]

Regardless of social class, British civilians carried on. They had intense worries about survival, but as time went on, the ordinariness of life's continuing took over. There was an extraordinary combination of horror and frightfulness; coping with the situation and, if one survived, life going on. Survival was a form of victory.

IX

The Myth, the Reality

"Our power to cope with fear"

THE TOLL on the British capital during the eight months of the Blitz was heavy. On its first night, September 7, 1940, more than 400 people were killed, more than 1,600 seriously injured, and many thousands were made homeless. The fires that night were the greatest London had ever experienced, including those of the Great Fire of September 2–6, 1666. In September and October 1940 alone, there were more than 13,000 fires. By the time the Blitz ended in the early hours of May 11, 1941, 18,291 tons of high explosive bombs had killed a total of 28,556 Londoners and 25,578 were seriously enough injured to require hospital care.[1] These figures were nevertheless a small percentage of the millions who lived in London.

Although the Blitz was a terrible experience for Londoners, Hitler failed to destroy London physically and to destroy the morale of its residents. Nor did the Germans deliver blows harsh enough so that the British sued for peace. Obviously the barrage of Nazi air raids caused much chaos, confusion, and disruption, but the British ability to wage war was far less damaged than Hitler had every reason to expect. If not very clearly and with much difficult fighting yet to come, it now appeared, perhaps for the first time, that the Axis were less likely to win the war. Or to put it another way, that Britain would not lose the war. As Churchill had remarked as early as the previous June, "Hitler will have to break us in this Island or lose the war."[2]

Even if the Blitz was a turning point in the war, I do not mean to suggest a triumphalist interpretation. In terms of damage and death, London, as well as other parts of Britain, paid a very heavy price. There had not been a previous raid of such intensity. If the United Kingdom were to break, it might well have been on the basis of the assault that first night, September 7, 1940. In the East End there were moments when the panic became quite intense and the considerable exodus might have become a rout. The fear of the bombing was immense. When it became clear that this was a heavier raid than any that had taken place before, the fear became virtually palpable. Many may have just managed to get through that first night of very heavy bombing. Over the first weekend, the nerve and spirit of those in the East End came close to breaking.

But then it became increasingly possible to survive the succeeding nights, even with the lack of sleep and the destruction not only of buildings but of so much that allowed a city to function. Human beings demonstrated their ability to put up with terror, as long as it didn't kill them.

The Blitz marked an introduction of modern terror on a large scale. Everyone on the home front was now at risk. Modern wars are fought by ordinary people. Yet in modern times, up through the First World War, most European civilians were generally not in danger of losing their lives – even if they might have experienced various deprivations. That was certainly not true in the Second World War, most notably for the 6 million Jews killed in the Holocaust, but also for other civilian victims, of both Axis and Allied bombing raids, who in their thousands experienced terror and death from bombs. Although those killed in the London Blitz were a very small proportion of the civilians killed in the war, they were among the first to experience such extensive and continual bombardment. Their situation meets the definition of terrorism provided by the former United Nations Secretary-General Kofi Annan: "It is intended to cause harm to civilians or non-combatants hence the purpose of such an act, by its nature or context, is to intimidate a population, or to compel a government or an international organization to do or to abstain from doing an act."[3]

There had been various preludes to the Blitz in London, such as the bombing of Warsaw and Rotterdam. Those attacks, however, were much more a part of a specific military campaign (although the Blitz, too, was originally intended in part to be a preparation for the invasion of Britain). Devastating as terror might be, the experience of the Blitz also demonstrates that it is very unlikely to be effective – albeit at an extremely high price for British civilians. Other cities were bombed during the war, but no city other than London was bombed so often for eight months, from September through May. Except for November 2, London was bombed every day for almost two months. After that, the city was bombed less frequently, but some of the raids were devastating, such as that of December 29. Then on May 10, the last day of the London Blitz, the Germans inflicted the heaviest bombing of all, resulting in almost 1,500 deaths.

As Hitler and Goering discovered, terror in itself is not likely to achieve the objects of those who practise it. The Japanese might well have continued to fight after the atomic bombs fell on Hiroshima and Nagasaki if their government had so decided. The Spaniards, after the bombing of trains in Madrid on March 11, 2004, would probably not have taken dramatic steps against their government if it had determined to retain its troops in Iraq. Terror is frequently counterproductive and strengthens the resolve of those who are attacked. Countries lose wars, but not because of terror. The London Blitz was a major modern example of terror failing to alter a nation's actions, failing to produce a groundswell for peace with Germany.

The most powerful evidence of what happened during the Blitz is the testimony of the people themselves, as they coped. Reactions of course were very different and the degree of terror varied. Many of the young, not surprisingly, found life incredibly exciting under the bombing (disasters – if one survives – can be defining and deeply memorable moments). The Blitz took place where one lived, in familiar territory, yet at the same time it was a transformation of one's world. There were temptations to hysteria; there were temptations to loot and pillage. At the time, such events tended to be kept out of the news (the censors forbade the publication of photographs of dead bodies or dismembered limbs). Looking back, in the course of revisionist history, the distressing aspects of the Blitz might be overemphasized.

Angus Calder has remarked about the Blitz (not just in London but elsewhere in Britain) that "no archive of such abundance exists for any other 'major event' in British history."[4] Except for dated letters and diaries (though even they may have been "touched up"), it's difficult to be sure when a particular memory was committed to paper. My original hypothesis had been that those accounts written closer to the event, under the impact of the war still going on, might be likely to be more heroic, conforming to the idea of "the myth of the Blitz." Myths are not necessarily falsehoods but might be transformations of experiences, making them emblematic and memorable – and possibly misrepresenting them. They provide a roadway for historical stories to enter the collective memory of a society. The word "myth" also has the implication of an exaggeration or indeed something that is untruthful. Whether the experience of the Blitz was heroic or not, it was certainly memorable and likely to be the most dramatic event in the lives of many of those who experienced it. Yet it is not clear to me that there were changes over the years in how the participants thought about their experiences. It also does not necessarily follow that the memory recorded immediately after an event, although obviously fresher, is more or less true than a memory put down much later. For some time after the war, the expectation was that people were heroic. This both conformed with and was reinforced by the British self-conception, their sense of irony and understatement.

As Vincent Sheean noted, one defining characteristic of the British people is the very high value they place on not seeming to be disturbed by disastrous events. One might also venture to suggest that this is the positive side of elements of E. M. Forster's well-known comment in *Notes on the English Character* that the British have undeveloped hearts (suppress emotions, do not say what you really think). Much of the population was convulsed by fear on September 7, 1940. But much of the population refused to reveal that fear, to say what they were really thinking. I don't think it is possible to overestimate the importance of this in explaining why the British survived.

To take but one example, Barbara Nixon acted as an air warden with calmness in a very stressful situation. Was she also, like others who recounted their experiences, doing her bit to contribute to the myth of the Blitz? Is it that everyone acted well (which was clearly untrue), or that everything went smoothly (also untrue)? If the myth is that people coped with varying degrees of success, then the myth is true. What is also true is that out of adversity eventually Britain moved on to victory. But the myth of the Blitz is something more. It became a construct that the British people, through their united heroism on the home front, had proved themselves worthy of being much better treated by their government.

National character is a slippery concept. It does not mean that one national group has any superiority over another. Though as legitimately terrified as anyone might be with bombs coming down and threatening one with death and injury, the British style, with many exceptions, was to hide fear and to attempt to rise above it; as best they could, they treated the attacks with irony and contempt. No doubt it is a common human tendency, but the way the British handled the situation fitted in easily with their conception of themselves. There is a certain almost self-conscious turning inward for sustenance, with the emphasis not so much on the assault itself but on how the people themselves reacted to what was increasingly seen as a "People's War." There was an emphasis, using the emblematic word of the time, on "coping." Another famous phrase that emerged was "London Can Take It." Although there was a desire for revenge, the primary reaction was concentration on Londoners' ability to survive, to pick up the pieces, to continue with as close a semblance to ordinary life as possible, the delivery of milk, the delivery of mail, the going to work. Despite the failures of government, there was fundamentally a long-lasting government structure and, while far from perfect, a tradition of participatory democracy that ultimately provided an infrastructure that enabled the populace to deal with the situation created by the heavy bombing over many days.

The heroic version of the myth of the Blitz argues that all behaved well and calmly, that it brought everyone together through experiences that all shared. This is clearly an exaggeration and has been rightly challenged – but the challengers may well have gone too far in the other direction, overemphasizing failures and bad behaviour. But if the myth of the Blitz is considered at its more modest level, then I believe that it has a fair amount of validity. Innumerable commentators at the time pointed out the great growth of friendliness and how much more the traditionally stand-offish British now spoke to one another, shared their experiences of the war on the home front. Although there were many exceptions, there was generally a much greater sense of community at all levels. Ideas of class, to a degree, it might be said, went underground. There was a sense that the British people, moving out of the bitter years of the Depression, came together to fight the Nazis. Churchill – and particularly his oratory – played a central role in this development. No doubt the Blitz was a major factor, but not the only one. The desperate need to fight Hitler existed whether or not Britain was bombed. But the myth in its strongest form argues that the Blitz created a unified people, no longer with internal divisions, who came together to win the war.

And a further aspect of the myth is that the war experience was an important factor in the postwar rise of the welfare state. After the First World War, the people of Britain had been promised "Homes Fit for Heroes," but that hadn't happened. During the Blitz, the people behaved so well that at the end of the war, they deserved a welfare state.[5] I believe this view has merit, but there may have also been an element of contrition involved. Viola Bawtree vividly expressed, both in a religious and also a wider political context, the disgraceful failure of those who should have done more to deal with the consequences of the bombing of civilians:

> I believe that possibly God allowed such horrors, including the insecurity of shelters, so that men & women should realise to the full that this sort of thing must be abolished for all time, & that no amount of deep digging will make people immune from the peril. Only, why is not more horror & destruction allowed to happen to the homes of those in high places, who are far more responsible for allowing bombers to be created than are the poor people in the East End?[6]

The role of the Blitz in the making of the welfare state lay in negatives. The government was not prepared for the needs of Londoners on that first weekend in September. There were not adequate plans for the living, whose lives were so dramatically altered by the bombing. A few days later, the tragedy at the South Hallsville School underlined the inadequacies of pre-war planning and of the immediate response of the authorities. As Ritchie Calder in particular and as Richard Titmuss in general made apparent, the government needed to take a much more proactive role in shaping how help would have to be administered. In addition, critics also stressed that the burden of the government's mistakes regarding civil defence fell most heavily on the working classes. These failures helped shape the Beveridge Report of 1942, which argued for a vastly expanded provision by the state of social services for all. The idea of the general responsibility of government, of society, for its members, from "cradle to grave," was moved forward in significant ways by the events of September 7.

After that day, with some difficulty and the passing of time, the national government committed itself to deal far more thoroughly with the human and physical devastation of the raids. In an emblematic way, this is summed up by the account of an Anglican clergyman from Hackney, H. A. Wilson, the vicar of St Augustine's, Haggerston, writing very soon after the events he describes. On the 7th, after a lunch at the Athenaeum, a well-known club in central London (particularly for distinguished figures with a serious bent of mind), Wilson took a bus back to his parish. He then exercised his dog, Mick, on a cricket pitch on the roof of his church hall, even though the sirens had sounded signalling an air raid.

> I carried a deck-chair out on to the asphalt playground, gave Mick the ball and old cricket-stump to play with, settled down in the sunshine with *The Times* crossword-puzzle and kept a weather-eye on the blue heavens above me. After a time I saw small round white clouds appear, as if from nowhere; heard distant sounds as though made by a door banging in the wind. … I saw a number of silvery white moths, circling and climbing, zooming and falling.

As the raid intensified, the vicar's aura of serenity faded and he tried to keep up the spirits of his parishioners in the church hall. "Hoping (I fear vainly) that I did not look as frightened as I felt. … I had no hope of living through that night; I merely sat and waited to be blown to bits or crushed to death. … I was frightened as I had never been before." But then the resolution in the very next sentence:

> Now we in East London have by force of circumstances, grown more accustomed to fear. … We have also discovered that it is in our power to cope with fear, and that it is neither a fatal disease or a thing to be ashamed of. We know now that the really brave person is not he or she who is unafraid; but he or she who is sick with fear, and yet "gets on with the job."

> ... We in Haggerston seemed to grow several years older in the space of that Saturday night at the end of September's first week; when the long fires raged by the river ... when the sky looked like the Day of Judgement, made one think of the Book of Revelation, when at last London learned what is meant by a Blitz.[7]

On the first day of the Blitz in London, as on September 11, 2001, "ordinary" people, in the wrong place at the wrong time, died. September 7, 1940 also heralded a series of events crucial to the history of Britain. Both days, 61 years apart, were marked by death and destruction, but they also provided evidence of our ability to survive as human beings.

Notes

1 The Beginning

The subtitle is the epigraph from Ritchie Calder, *The Lesson of London* (London, 1941), p. 128. This was the third volume in the Searchlight Books series edited by George Orwell and T. R. Fyvel. The series was devoted to considering various problems that needed to be solved either during the war or in the society that would come after it. Its rather grandiose announcement ran, "It is the aim of SEARCHLIGHT BOOKS to do all in their power to criticise and kill what is rotten in Western civilisation and supply constructive ideas for the difficult period ahead of us. The series ... will stress Britain's international and imperial responsibilities and the aim of a planned Britain at the head of a greater and freer British Commonwealth." Orwell himself wrote the first and the most famous book in the series, *The Lion and the Unicorn*. In it he enunciated his fiercely socialist patriotism, with its depiction of England as a family with the wrong members in control. He felt based on his experience of Spain that there would probably need to be a transformation of society, through bloody revolution if necessary, if Britain were to win the war. Ten varied titles were published in the series until it was stopped by the destruction of its paper supply when the printers were bombed in Portsmouth. (See Bernard Crick, *George Orwell* (Boston, 1980), p. 273.) Ritchie Calder is the father of Angus Calder, author of *The People's War* (London, 1969).

1 Quoted from *Time* (n.d.) in Edward Rothstine, "Contemplating Churchill," *Smithsonian*, March 2005, p. 98.

2 Ultimately, there were far more British military dead: 294,000.

3 Eyal Ginio, "Transmitting the Agony of a Besieged Population: Edirne (Adrianople) in Ottoman Propaganda during the Balkan Wars, 1912–1913," paper delivered at Metropolitan Catastrophes Conference, July 13, 2004.

4 See Susan R. Grayzel, "'A Promise of Terror to Come': Air Power

and the Destruction of Cities in British Imagination and Experience, 1908–1939." In *Cities into Battlefields: The Metropolitan Dimension of Total War* (forthcoming).

5 TV broadcast on the day.

6 *New York Times*, July 9, 2005.

II Preparing for War

1 Quoted in H. Montgomery Hyde and G. R. Falkiner Nuttall, *Air Defence and the Civil Population* (London, 1938), p. 3.

2 The Labour candidate turned a 14,000 Tory majority into a 5,000 Labour majority. This was universally taken as an endorsement of pacifism while in fact it was more likely to have been motivated by the government's policy toward the unemployed. See A. J. P. Taylor, *English History, 1914–1945* (Oxford, 1965), p. 367.

3 I owe this point to Sir Michael Howard.

4 Although the Blitz itself did not fulfil Wells's depiction, one might argue that the millions dead and the atrocities committed in the Second World War did. See Niall Ferguson, *The War of the World: Twentieth-Century Conflict and the Descent of the West* (New York, 2006).

5 See Grayzel, "'A Promise of Terror to Come.'"

6 Bertrand Russell quoted in Ken Young and Patricia L. Garside, *Metropolitan London* (London, 1982), p. 222.

7 Quoted in Blitz Web Exhibition at museumoflondon.org.uk.

8 Constantine FitzGibbon, *The Blitz* (London, 1957), p. 7.

9 Terence H. O'Brien, *Civil Defence* (London, 1955), pp. 120–1.

10 Quoting memorandum no. 4 (1st edn), "Air Raid Wardens," March 4, 1937, O'Brien, *Civil Defence*, p. 72. O'Brien provides the information used here on the establishment of the service.

11 FitzGibbon, *The Blitz*, p. 64.

12 As usual, the question was who would pay, local authorities or the government, and how the costs would be divided. Ultimately, the government pledged 5.5 to 8 million pounds for the air raid warden service, to which the local authorities were expected to contribute from about a sixth up to 40 per cent. O'Brien, *Civil Defence*, p. 94.

13 Ibid., p. 96.

14 Figure on display, Cabinet War Rooms, London.

15 O'Brien, *Civil Defence*, p. 128.

16 FitzGibbon, *The Blitz*, p. 19.

17 Quoted in ibid.
18 See Sir Harold Scott, *Your Obedient Servant* (London, 1959).
19 Ibid., p. 120.
20 O'Brien, *Civil Defence*, p. 19.
21 Quoting "The ARP Committee's First Report," O'Brien, *Civil Defence*, p. 19.
22 Winston G. Ramsey, ed., *The Blitz Then and Now* (London, 1988), vol. 1, p. 412.
23 See www.fortunecity.co.uk/meltingpot/oxford/330/shel/shel2.html.
24 John Lukacs, *Five Days in London, May 1940* (New Haven, Conn., 1999), p. 191. Hugh Sebag-Montefiore in *Dunkirk* (Cambridge, Mass., 2006) cites two different sets of figures, one with this figure of 338,226 as the total of British and French evacuated, and the other for both as 315,567 (p. 541). He also states that among the British there were 11,014 killed or who died of wounds, 14,074 wounded and 41,338 either missing or prisoners of war (p. 506).
25 Quoted in the unpublished memoirs of Major-General Sir Alec Bishop, "Look Back with Pleasure," vol. 1, p. 69, 98/18/1, Imperial War Museum, London. Hereafter Imperial War Museum.
26 The rest of the poem:

This is the war we always knew,
When every county keeps her own,
When Kent stands sentry in the lane,
And Fenland guards her dyke and drain,
Cornwall, her cliffs of stone;

When from the Cinque Ports and the Wight,
From Plymouth Sound and Bristol Town,
There comes a noise that breaks our sleep,
Of the deep calling to the deep
Where the ships go up and down,

And near and far across the world
Hold open wide the water-gates,
And all the tall adventurers come
Homeward to England, and Drake's drum
Is beaten through the Straits.

This is the war that we have known
And fought in every hundred years,
Our sword, upon the last, steep path,

Forged by the hammer of our wrath
    On the anvil of our fears.

Send us, O God, the will and power
    To do as we have done before;
The men that ride the sea and air
Are the same men their fathers were
    To fight the English war.

And send, O God, an English peace –
    Some sense, some decency, perhaps
Some justice, too, if we are able,
With no sly jackals round our table,
    Cringing for blood-stained scraps;

No dangerous dreams of wishful men
    Whose homes are safe, who never feel
The flying death that swoops and stuns,
The kisses of the curtseying guns
    Slavering their streets with steel;

No dreams, Lord God, but vigilance,
    That we may keep, by might and main,
Inviolate seas, inviolate skies; –
But, if another tyrant rise,
    Then we shall fight again.

The table of contents of the issue included books on the war such as one on Dunkirk, as well as traditional fare: new novels including one by Warwick Deeping, new detective stories, and a book on the Tudor theory of Kingship by the American historian, Franklin Le Van Baumer.

27 Ministry of Home Security, *Front Line* (London, 1942).

28 Virginia Cowles, *Looking for Trouble* (New York, 1941), pp. 414–15.

29 A. J. P. Taylor, *The Second World War: An Illustrated History* (1975; reprint, New York, 1979), p. 69.

30 See Stephen Brooks, *Bomber* (London, 1983), p. 23.

31 Mrs M. E. Stevenson, Diary 1940, 86/546/1, Department of Documents, Imperial War Museum.

32 Paul Overy, *The Battle of Britain* (New York, 2000), p. 91.

33 Mrs M. (Molly) Fenlon, Diary, p. 1, 01/3/1, Imperial War Museum.

34 Miss P. Warner, Diary, 95/14/1, Imperial War Museum.
35 Cajus Bekker, *The Luftwaffe War Diaries* (London, 1964), p. 171.
36 Taylor, *The Second World War*, pp. 69–70.
37 The British and the Americans would ultimately draw the wrong conclusion from this, that the Germans did not destroy British production and morale because they did not bomb enough. So they later inflicted their much more destructive raids against Germany, again without accomplishing either object, although there might have been tactical achievements.

III September 7, 1940

1 I haven't been able to discover when the term "Black Saturday" started to be used. It was also employed to mark the day a German U-boat sank the *Royal Oak* in Scapa Flow in October 1940, actually very early on a Sunday morning.
2 O'Brien, *Civil Defence*, p. 587.
3 Mary Eleanor Allan papers, 95/8/7, Imperial War Museum.
4 Ramsey, *The Blitz Then and Now*, vol. 2, p. 45.
5 Virginia Cowles, *Looking for Trouble* (New York, 1941), p. 415.
6 Harold Nicolson, *The Diaries and Letters*, vol. 2: *The War Years 1939–1945*, ed. Nigel Nicolson (New York, 1967), p. 111.
7 Richard Hough and Denis Richards, *The Battle of Britain* (New York, 1989), p. 258.
8 Miss H. P. L. Mott, Diary, Sept. 7, 1940, 97/14/1, Imperial War Museum.
9 Joanna Mack and Steve Humphries, *London at War: The Making of Modern London, 1939–1945* (London, 1985), p. 40.
10 Viola Bawtree, Diary of 1940–1, Sept. 7, 1940, 91/5/1, Imperial War Museum.
11 Jack Graham Wright, Memoir, pp. 6–7, 97/19/1, Imperial War Museum.
12 The Rev. B. P. Mohan, Diary, 96/49/1, Imperial War Museum.
13 Robert Westall, *Children of the Blitz* (London, 1987), p. 101.
14 This 1940 British film was known as *Angel Street* in the United States, and was remade in Hollywood under the English title in 1944.
15 Bryan Forbes, *Notes for a Life* (London, 1974), pp. 53–4.
16 Leslie Jerman to Rob Kirk, April 21, 1990, p. 1, 67/262/1, Imperial War Museum.
17 Copy of Jo Oakman's Diary, Sept. 7, 1940, in vol. 1, p. 9, 91/20/1, Imperial War Museum.

18 Barbara Nixon, *Raiders Overhead: A Diary of the London Blitz* (1943; revised edn, London, 1980), p. 13.
19 Jane Waller and Michael Vaughan-Rees, *Blitz: The Civilian War, 1940–45* (London, 1990), pp. 12–13.
20 F. W. Hurd, "Blitz over London," 80/30/1, Imperial War Museum.
21 Jack Graham Wright, Memoir, pp. 7–9, 97/19/1, Imperial War Museum.
22 Alfred Price, *Blitz on Britain: The Bomber Attacks on the United Kingdom, 1939–1945* (London, 1977), pp. 78–9.
23 See Yoel Sheridan, *From Here to Obscurity* (London, 2001).
24 Angus Calder, *The People's War* (London, 1969), p. 164.
25 Bernard Kops, *The World Is a Wedding* (New York, 1963), pp. 63–7.
26 Jim Wolveridge, *Ain't It Grand* (London, 1981), pp. 69–71.
27 Eve Hostettler, ed., *The Island at War: Memories of War-time Life on the Isle of Dogs, East London* (London, 1990), David Marson, p. 13.
28 Anon. quoted in ibid., pp. 13–14.
29 Quoted in Waller and Vaughan-Rees, *Blitz*, pp. 13–14.
30 Hostettler, *The Island at War*, pp. 14–15.
31 Lilian Burnett, in Paul Schweitzer, ed., *Londoners Remember Living through the Blitz* (n.p., 1991), p. 19.
32 Mervyn Haisman and L. E. Snellgrove, *Dear Merv … Dear Bill* (Llandysul, Dyfed: Gomer Press, 1992), pp. 83–7

IV The Second Raid

1 Price, *Blitz on Britain*, pp. 79, 92. See also Basil Collier, *The Battle of Britain* (London, 1962), p. 134.
2 Tom Harrisson, *Living through the Blitz* (New York, 1976), pp. 59–61.
3 Mack and Humphries, *London at War*, p. 41.
4 Eric Sevareid, *Not So Wild a Dream* (1946; reprint, Columbia, Mo., 1976), pp. 172–3.
5 Diana Forbes-Robertson and Roger W. Straus, Jr, eds, *War Letters from Britain* (New York, 1941), pp. 132–3.
6 FitzGibbon, *The Blitz*, pp. 58–9.
7 Jennifer Golden, *Hackney at War* (London, 1995), pp. 122–3.
8 FitzGibbon, *The Blitz*, p. 59.
9 Anne Shepperd, "Typed Extracts from a Diary of the Blitz of London–1940," p. 4, 95/13/1, Imperial War Museum.

10 FitzGibbon, *The Blitz*, p. 63.
11 Mary Price, quoted in Waller and Vaughan-Rees, *Blitz*, pp. 25–6.
12 Mack and Humphries, *London at War*, p. 41.
13 Violet I. Regan, "The German Blitzkrieg, Saturday September 7th 1940" (8 pp.), 88/10/1, Imperial War Museum. Published in a somewhat different version in Ben Wicks, *Waiting for the All Clear* (London, 1990), pp. 56–9.
14 Robert Baltrop, transcript of Thames TV interview, pp. 4–11, 67/262/1, Imperial War Museum.
15 S. M. S. Woodcock, "Memoir," 87/36/1, Imperial War Museum.
16 George Beardmore, *Civilians at War* (London, 1984), p. 80.
17 Mea Allan to Mrs A. M. Chalmers, Sept. 7, 1940, 95/8/7, Imperial War Museum.
18 Doris Pierce, *Memories of the Civilian War 1939–1945* (London, 1996), pp. 19–22, 32.
19 Ernest Raymond, *Please You, Draw Near* (London, 1969), p. 74.
20 Sgt A. C. O'Shea of the 2nd Battalion the King's Royal Rifle Corps, manuscript memoir, 1984 The Second World War Experience Centre, Leeds.
21 See Dennis Arundell, *The Story of Sadler's Wells* (Newton Abbot, 1978), p. 217, and Peter Stansky and William Abrahams, *London's Burning* (Stanford, 1994).
22 Price, *Blitz on Britain*, p. 78.
23 William Sansom, *The Blitz: Westminster at War* (1947; reprint, Oxford, 1990), pp. 26–8.
24 Mrs Ernestine Hunt Cotton, "Journal for Penelope," photocopy of typed manuscript, pp. 136–7, 93/3/1, Imperial War Museum.
25 Joan Wyndham, *Love Lessons: A Wartime Diary* (London, 1985), pp. 113–17.
26 N. Bosanquet to her mother, Sept. 16(?), 1940, 81/33/1, Imperial War Museum. The date of her letter has been obscured by the rust of a paper clip; it may be as late as September 16 as the date on the letter is unlikely to be the 6th which is what it looks like. Yet I am taking the liberty of including it because it so vividly documents the change of mood caused by an air raid, and the ultimate resolution to put up with it.
27 Nixon, *Raiders Overhead*, p. 10.
28 Copy of Josephine May Oakman's diary, Sept. 10, 1940; Ernest W. J. Nicholson writing about her, May 7, 1977, 91/20/1, Imperial War Museum.

29 E. M. Forster to Christopher Isherwood, Sept. 11, 1940, CI826, Isherwood Papers, Huntington Library, San Marino, Calif.
30 P. N. Furbank, *E. M. Forster* (New York, 1978), vol. 2, p. 239.
31 The Rev. B. P. Mohan manuscript diary, 96/49/1, Imperial War Museum.
32 Colin Perry, *Boy in the Blitz* (1972; reprint, Stroud, 2000), pp. 110–15.
33 Viola Bawtree, Sept. 8, 9, 1940, 91/5/1, Imperial War Museum.
34 Mack and Humphries, *London at War*, pp. 41–3.

V Civil Defence

1 Other units were Report and Control; Messengers; First-Aid Posts; Emergency Mortuary; Food Treatment; Decontamination; Women's Voluntary Services; Gas Identification; and Post Raid. Anon., *Hampstead at War* (London, 1946), pp. 34–7.
2 Tony Kushner, *The Persistence of Prejudice: Antisemitism in British Society during the Second World War* (Manchester, 1989), pp. 53–4.
3 Vincent Sheean, *Between the Thunder and the Sun* (New York, 1943), p. 234.
4 See Geoffrey Field, "Underground in Darkest London: The Blitz 1940–41," *International Labor and Working Class History*, no. 63 (Fall 2002), p. 12.
5 *Jewish Chronicle*, Sept. 13, 1940, pp. 1, 10.
6 Mass Observation File 392, quoted in Arthur Marwick, *The Home Front* (London, 1976), p. 49.
7 Lady Violet Bonham Carter, "Air-Raid Wardens' Claims," in Fiona Glass and Philip Marsden-Smedley, eds, *Articles of War: The Spectator Book of World War II* (London, 1989), Nov. 8, 1940, pp. 146–7.
8 Anon., quoted in Howard Bloch, ed., *Black Saturday: The First Day of the Blitz: East London Memories of September 7th 1940* (London, 1984), pp. 24–5.
9 FitzGibbon, *The Blitz*, pp. 64–5.
10 Nixon, *Raiders Overhead*, p. 53.
11 FitzGibbon, *The Blitz*, p. 55.
12 Nixon, *Raiders Overhead*, pp. 10–11.
13 Ibid., p. 26.
14 D. Lord, Memoir, 91/19/1, Imperial War Museum, London.
15 Quoted in Price, *Blitz on Britain*, p. 92.

16 Quoted in FitzGibbon, *The Blitz*, p. 48.
17 Hannen Swaffer, "Jack Maynard," in Derek Tangye, ed., *Went the Day Well* (London, 1942), pp. 115–16.
18 Mack and Humphries, *London at War*, p. 55.
19 Frank Shaw and Joan Shaw, *We Remember the Blitz* (Hinkley, 1990), p. 49.
20 F. W. Hurd, "Blitz over London," Dec. 1940, 80/30/1, Imperial War Museum.
21 Ibid.
22 These quotations from Cyril Demarne, *The London Blitz: A Fireman's Tale* (1980; reprint, London, 1991), pp. 17–26.
23 FitzGibbon, *The Blitz*, pp. 48, 56. His interviews took place in 1957.
24 Ibid., p. 50.
25 This and previous quotation from A. P. Herbert, *Independent Member* (New York, 1951), pp. 138–9.
26 A. P. Herbert, *The Thames* (London, 1966), p. 165.
27 Waller and Vaughan-Rees, *Blitz*, pp. 20–1.
28 Swaffer, "Jack Maynard," p. 114.
29 W. B. Regan, "Document 1," pp. 2–6, edited by his daughter, Ann Regan Atherton, in 1989, 88/10/1, Imperial War Museum. His wife Violet's account of the bombing appeared in chapter IV.
30 Ritchie Calder, *The Lesson of London* (London, 1941), p. 12.

VI Picking up the Pieces

1 Burnett, *Londoners Remember*, p. 27.
2 Nixon, *Raiders Overhead*, p. 18.
3 Mack and Humphries, *London at War*, p. 43.
4 Haisman and Snellgrove, *Dear Merv … Dear Bill*, p. 87.
5 Quoted in Basil Woon, *Hell Came to London* (London, 1941), p. 16.
6 T. C. G. James, *The Battle of Britain* (London, 2000), pp. 239–43.
7 B. H. Liddell Hart, *History of World War II* (London, 1970), p. 104.
8 Many of the details of the raid are from Francis K. Mason, *Battle over Britain* (New York, 1970), pp. 358–69.
9 Stephen Brooks, *Bomber* (London, 1983), p. 25.
10 *Daily Express*, September 9, 1940.
11 Field Marshal Lord Alanbrooke, *War Diaries 1939–1945*, ed. Alex Danchev and Daniel Tolman (London, 2001), pp. 105–12, for all statements made by Alanbrooke quoted in this chapter.

12 Tim Clayton and Phil Craig, *Finest Hour* (London, 1999), p. 296.
13 Richard Collier, *1940: The World in Flames* (London, 1961), p. 174.
14 See INF 1/250, National Archives, Kew, London.
15 See Marion Yass, *This Is Your War* (London, 1983), pp. 12–21.
16 CAB 65/9, National Archives, Kew, London.
17 Robertson was working for *PM*, the liberal New York City newspaper I grew up with – I rather hope that at the age of eight I was aware enough to read his dispatches.
18 Ben Robertson, *I Saw England* (New York, 1941), pp. 119–23.
19 Edward R. Murrow, *This Is London* (1941; reprint, New York, 1985), pp. 157–61.
20 Sheean, *Between the Thunder and the Sun*, pp. 224–9.
21 *The New Yorker Book of War Pieces* (New York, 1947), p. 62
22 Edward R. Murrow Collection, Digital Collections and Archives, Tufts University, Medford, Mass.
23 See the introductory note in chapter I.
24 See Ritchie Calder, "Sleep We Must," *New Statesman*, Sept. 14, 1940, pp. 252–3.
25 Dorothy Ratcliffe to Jack, Sept. 10, 1940, Imperial War Museum, letter reproduced in *The Home Front 1939–1945* (London, n.d.).
26 Ramsey, *Blitz Then and Now*, vol. 2, p. 77.
27 Calder, *The Lesson of London*, pp. 17–21.
28 According to Mack and Humphries, *London at War*, p. 50. Yet another account states: "The school suffered a direct hit, causing the biggest civilian disaster of the 2nd World War – as many as 400 people died under the rubble" (webpage of East End Talking). In *The Lesson of London*, Calder claims about 450 people died. However, official figures recorded a total of 73 people killed, less than at some other "incidents" (Ramsey, *Blitz Then and Now*, vol. 2, p. 77).
29 Ramsey, *Blitz Then and Now*, vol. 2, p. 411.
30 Calder, *The Lesson of London*, p. 128.
31 *The Times*, Sept. 11, 1940, p. 4.
32 Glyn Maxwell, *The Sugar Mile* (Boston, 2005), pp. 130–1.
33 Winifred Eden-Green and Alan Eden-Green, *Testament of a Peace Lover: Letters from Vera Brittain* (London, 1988), p. 55.
34 Richard M. Titmuss, *Problems of Social Policy* (London, 1950), p. 254. In a footnote Titmuss points out that, from the context, in this instance "poor relief" meant "operating the emergency services for the homeless."
35 Ibid., p. 255.

36 Those who had left London were not necessarily in good shape. Frances Partridge, at her house Ham Spray in Wiltshire, put up some London refugees. "They looked better after sleep. Lack of sleep was their great trouble. ... The father of the family was still in a highly nervous state, and rolled his eyes like a shying horse as he described how he thought every bomb was going to hit him." Frances Partridge, *A Pacifist's War* (New York, 1978), p. 59.
37 F. R. Barry, *Period of My Life* (London, 1970), pp. 132–3.
38 Graham Greene, *The Ministry of Fear* (1943; reprint, New York, 1982), p. 247.
39 Caroline Lang, *Keep Smiling Through: Women in the Second World War* (Cambridge, 1989), p. 16. These numbers vary somewhat from account to account but there is no doubt that there were millions of houses destroyed.
40 "East End at War," *Picture Post*, Sept. 28, 1940.
41 Mass Observation File 431 quoted in Marwick, *The Home Front*, p. 49.
42 Quoted in Marwick, *The Home Front*, p. 69.
43 Reginald William Bell, *The Bull's Eye* (London, 1943), p. 50.
44 Ibid., p. 52.
45 Forbes-Robertson and Straus, *War Letters from Britain*, p. 134.
46 Ibid., p. 141.
47 Elizabeth Bowen, *The Heat of the Day* (New York, 1949), p. 98.
48 Elizabeth Bowen, *Collected Impressions* (London, 1950), p. 217.
49 Elizabeth Bowen, *Seven Winters and Afterthoughts* (New York, 1972), pp. 233–4.
50 Elizabeth Bowen, *Ivy Gripped the Steps* (New York, 1946), p. 233.
51 Margaret Kennedy, *Where Stands a Wingèd Sentry* (New Haven, Conn., 1941), pp. 210, 212–13.
52 Bloch, *Black Saturday*, pp. 9, 22.
53 For Intelligence Report and troops, see Philip Ziegler, *London at War 1939–1945* (1995; reprint, London, 2002), p. 176.
54 *Winston S. Churchill: His Complete Speeches 1897–1963* (New York, 1974), vol. 6, pp. 6276–7.

VII The People's War

1 Quoted in Winston S. Churchill, *Their Finest Hour* (Boston, 1949), p. 328.
2 Alanbrooke, *War Diaries 1939–1945*, p. 107.

3 Diana Brinton Lee, "It Happened Like This," p. 39, P178, Imperial War Museum.
4 Glass and Marsden-Smedley, eds, *The Spectator Book*, p. 127.
5 Ibid., pp. 128–9.
6 Nigel Fountain, ed., *The Battle of Britain and the Blitz* (London, 2002), p. 58.
7 Sevareid, *Not So Wild a Dream*, p. 179.
8 Alanbrooke, *War Diaries 1939–1945*, pp. 105–12. Alanbrooke's latter comments were made between 1951 and 56 (p. xxxi).
9 Yass, *This Is Your War*, p. 33.
10 Cajust Bekker, *The Luftwaffe War Diaries* (London, 1964), p. 171.
11 Quoted in Bishop, "Look Back with Pleasure," p. 69.
12 Quoted, no source given, in Len Deighton and Max Hastings, *Battle of Britain* (London, 1980), p. 167.
13 Robert Wright, *Dowding and the Battle of Britain* (London, 1969), p. 184.
14 Quoted, no source given, in Ronald W. Clark, *Battle for Britain* (London, 1965), p. 142.
15 Irving L. Janis, *Air War and Emotional Stress: Psychological Studies of Bombing and Civilian Defense* (New York, 1951), p. 194.
16 Mack and Humphries, *London at War*, p. 58.
17 Alan Bennett, Peter Cook, Jonathan Miller and Dudley Moore, *The Complete Beyond the Fringe* (London, 1987), p. 77.
18 Sheean, *Between the Thunder and the Sun*, pp. 230–1.
19 Yass, *This Is Your War*, p. 33.
20 Sevareid, *Not So Wild a Dream*, p. 172.
21 John Langdon-Davies, *Nerves versus Nazis* (London, 1940).
22 The Trustees of the Mass Observation Archive, University of Sussex, Diarist 382.
23 Nixon, *Raiders Overhead*, p. 22.
24 Bell, *The Bull's Eye*, p. 50.
25 There is an interesting correction in the text, in that Jews was typed with a lower case j and then someone has capitalized the J by hand, perhaps indicating a slight increase in sensitivity.
26 All quotations from the indicated day in Paul Addison, ed., *The British People and World War II: Home Intelligence Reports on Opinion and Morale, 1940–1944* (Microfilm) (Brighton, 1979), Reel 1.
27 See Marwick, *The Home Front*, p. 50.
28 Frank Ball, in *Londoners Remember*, pp. 14–15.
29 Mack and Humphries, *London at War*, p. 52.

30 Ibid.

31 Richard L. Jackson to Constantine FitzGibbon, May 16, 1957, Constantine FitzGibbon Collection, Humanities Research Center, University of Texas, Austin. Figures from Stuart Hylton, *Their Darkest Hour* (London, 2001), pp. 187–9.

32 Taylor, *English History*, p. 600.

33 Sevareid, *Not So Wild a Dream*, pp. 173–5.

34 Ian McLaine, *Ministry of Morale* (London, 1979), p. 28. I owe this reference to Chris Hilliard.

35 Mark Holland to H-Albion, Sept. 23, 2004.

36 Mark Rawlinson, *British Writing in the Second World War* (Oxford, 2000), p. 142. I owe this reference to Chris Hilliard.

37 For a discussion of these issues, see Sonya O. Rose, *Which People's War?* (New York, 2003).

38 J. B. Priestley, *Postscripts* (London, 1940), pp. 67–9.

39 Shaw and Shaw, *We Remember the Blitz*, p. 159.

40 Harrisson, *Living through the Blitz*, p. 64.

41 Quoted in David Souden, *War of the Unknown Warriors* (London, 2005), p. 140. In part thanks to the fire-watchers, St Paul's miraculously survived, although its high altar was damaged the night of October 10.

42 Rebecca West, *Black Lamb and Grey Falcon* (New York, 1943), pp. 1131–2.

VIII An Ideal but Impermanent City

1 George Orwell, "Review of *War Begins at Home*," *Time and Tide*, March 2, 1940, in George Orwell, *A Patriot after All: 1940–1941*, vol. 12 of *The Complete Works* (London, 1998), pp. 17–18.

2 See Paul Addison, "Introduction," in Addison, *The British People and World War II.*

3 Ibid., pp. 192–3.

4 Nicola Beauman, Elizabeth Taylor's biographer, email to author, Aug. 14, 2005.

5 The Trustees of the Mass Observation Archive, University of Sussex, James Burbridge, Diary 5037 Sept. 7, 1940.

6 Orwell, *A Patriot after All*, pp. 254–6.

7 Quoted in Ramsey, *The Blitz Then and Now*, vol. 2, p. 65.

8 George Orwell, "War-time Diary" April 8, 1941, in Orwell, *A Patriot after All*, pp. 467–8.

9 "London Letter," in Orwell, *A Patriot after All*, pp. 355–6.
10 Julian Symons, *Notes from Another Country* (London, 1972), pp. 84–92.
11 Elizabeth Watson, *Don't Wait for It or Impressions of War, 1939–1941* (London, 1994), p. 9.
12 Vera Brittain, *England's Hour: An Autobiography 1939–1941* (London, 1981), p. 94.
13 Ibid., p. 120.
14 Ibid., pp. 122–3.
15 Ibid., p. 109.
16 Theodora FitzGibbon, *With Love* (London, 1982), pp. 58–9.
17 Quoted by Sarah Lyall, "Londoners, Remembering Crises Old and New, Just 'Get On With It,'" *New York Times*, July 11, 2005, p. 11.
18 FitzGibbon, *With Love*, p. 63
19 Molly Lefebure, "Night in the Front Line," in Anne Boston, ed., *Wave Me Goodbye: Stories of the Second World War* (London, 1999), pp. 56–7.
20 Leslie Jerman to Rob Kirk, April 21, 1990, 67/262/1, Imperial War Museum.
21 Ralph Ingersoll, *Report on England: November, 1940* (New York, 1940), pp. 5, 201–2.
22 See Edward Glover, "Notes on the Psychological Effects of War Conditions on the Civilian Population. III The 'Blitz,'" *International Journal of Psycho-Analysis*, 23 (1942), pp. 17–37.
23 Ibid., p. 28.
24 Melitta Schmideberg, "Some Observations on Individual Reactions to Air Raids," *International Journal of Psycho-Analysis*, 23 (1942), p. 147.
25 Ibid., p. 160.
26 Ibid., p. 175.
27 Janis, *Air War and Emotional Stress*, pp. 73–111; quotation on p. 111.
28 Anon., *Fire over London 1940–41* (1941; reprint, London, 1995), p. 3.

IX The Myth, the Reality

1 John Ray, *The Night Blitz 1940–1941* (London, 1996), p. 260.
2 David Dilks, ed., *The Diaries of Sir Alexander Cadogan* (London, 1971), p. 303 (June 15, 1940).

3 As quoted in the *Times Literary Supplement*, April 22, 2005, p. 27.
4 Angus Calder, *The Myth of the Blitz* (London, 1991), p. 119.
5 However, one could argue that the welfare state was shaped far more by forces in British society that went back through its history deep into the nineteenth century, but more immediately to the 1930s. And to what degree the welfare state actually fundamentally changed the British nation is an interesting question, but one outside the purview of this book.
6 Viola Bawtree, 91/1/1, Imperial War Museum.
7 H. A. Wilson, *Death over Haggerston* (London, 1941), pp. 121–5.

Index